Russian Arms Transfers to East Asia in the 1990s

Stockholm International Peace Research Institute

SIPRI is an independent international institute for research into problems of peace and conflict, especially those of arms control and disarmament. It was established in 1966 to commemorate Sweden's 150 years of unbroken peace.

The Institute is financed mainly by the Swedish Parliament. The staff and the Governing Board are international. The Institute also has an Advisory Committee as an international consultative body.

The Governing Board is not responsible for the views expressed in the publications of the Institute.

Governing Board

Professor Daniel Tarschys, Chairman (Sweden)
Dr Oscar Arias Sánchez (Costa Rica)
Sir Marrack Goulding (United Kingdom)
Dr Ryukichi Imai (Japan)
Dr Catherine Kelleher (United States)
Dr Marjatta Rautio (Finland)
Dr Lothar Rühl (Germany)
Dr Abdullah Toukan (Jordan)
The Director

Director

Dr Adam Daniel Rotfeld (Poland)

Russian Arms Transfers to East Asia in the 1990s

SIPRI Research Report No. 15

Alexander A. Sergounin and Sergey V. Subbotin

OXFORD UNIVERSITY PRESS
1999

Oxford University Press, Walton Street, Oxford OX2 6DP
Oxford New York
Athens Auckland Bangkok Bombay
Calcutta Cape Town Dar es Salaam Delhi
Florence Hong Kong Istanbul Karachi
Kuala Lumpur Madras Madrid Melbourne
Mexico City Nairobi Paris Singapore
Taipei Tokyo Toronto
and associated companies in
Berlin Ibadan

Oxford is a trade mark of Oxford University Press

Published in the United States
by Oxford University Press Inc., New York

British Library Cataloguing in Publication Data
Data available

Library of Congress Cataloging in Publication Data
Data available

ISBN 0–19–829576–6
ISBN 0–19–829577–4 (pbk.)

Typeset and originated by Stockholm International Peace Research Institute
Printed in Great Britain
on acid-free paper by
Biddles Ltd, Guildford and King's Lynn

Contents

Preface

In 1994–96 Alexander A. Sergounin carried out a research project entitled Arms Transfers and Security in East and Southeast Asia, sponsored by the United States Institute of Peace (USIP) and administered by the Stockholm International Peace Research Institute (SIPRI). A key role in the execution of this project was played by Dr Ian Anthony, then Leader of the SIPRI Arms Transfers Project, who provided useful advice for the preparation of earlier drafts of this research report. The report is both the end-product and a continuation of this project, with emphasis on Russia's role in the arms trade with countries of East Asia.

Arms and military technology transfers are one of the main instruments of Russia's security strategy in East Asia. Why does Russia lay emphasis on arms exports? What is its motivation? Is it an attempt to help the troubled domestic defence industry, a vehicle for alliance politics, a tool in the regional power struggle or something else? How are decisions on arms transfers taken in Russia? What are the legal and institutional frameworks? What are the programmes of military–technical cooperation with the East Asian nations? How do they affect the balance of power in the region? What are the security implications? This book addresses these questions.

There are some grounds for assuming that Russia relies on the arms trade not only because of domestic problems but also because of the lack of other effective instruments of policy towards East Asia. For this reason, it is important to make Russia, as well as China, an equal participant in regional multilateral institutions, thus eliminating the grounds for temptation to use destabilizing measures for self-affirmation in the area. Inclusive rather than exclusive policies and multilateralism rather than power politics can help to ensure that Russia and other regional actors are constructive and help to pave the way to establishing a cooperative security regime in East Asia.

It should be noted that this book was written in the mid-1990s, before the major economic crisis hit many of the East Asian economies. This, as well as the continuing crises and changes in Russia, will undoubtedly have an impact on some of the trends described here. While it could not document the dramatic developments of the last years of this decade, the book makes an important contribution to our understanding of the early phases of arms transfer policy in the new Russian Federation.

Adam Daniel Rotfeld
Director of SIPRI
October 1998

Acknowledgements

This volume is the result of several projects carried out in close cooperation and consultation with the Stockholm International Peace Research Institute (SIPRI). The work on this project was truly collegial: this report also reflects the results of previous studies conducted by Sergey V. Subbotin.

SIPRI, under its Director, Dr Adam Daniel Rotfeld, has provided invaluable help to the authors in many ways. The authors are indebted to Dr Ian Anthony, former Leader of the SIPRI Arms Transfers Project, who played a key role in execution of the project with the United States Institute of Peace (USIP) by being its principal consultant. The authors extend special thanks to Siemon T. Wezeman and Pieter D. Wezeman for their extensive and insightful comments and suggestions as well for sharing SIPRI Arms Transfers Project data with us.

It is a pleasant duty to mention here our gratitude to some colleagues who have helped us with especially useful advice or materials for this report. They include: Ambassador Michael Armacost, President, the Brookings Institution; Dr Frank Fischer, Professor of Political Science, Rutgers University; Dr Bates Gill, former Leader of the SIPRI Project on Security and Arms Control in East Asia; Dr Bjørn Møller, Leader of the Military Restructuring Project, Copenhagen Peace Research Institute (COPRI); Dr Jerry Segal, Senior Fellow, International Institute for Strategic Studies (IISS); Dr Dmitry Trenin, Research Fellow, Moscow Carnegie Centre; Digby Waller, Defence Economist, IISS; Dr Howard J. Wiarda, Professor of Foreign Policy Studies, University of Massachusetts; Håkan Wiberg, Director, COPRI; Susan Willett, former Research Fellow, COPRI; and Ruan Zongze, Deputy Director, World Politics Studies, China Institute of International Studies.

We would like to thank Eve Johansson for her sharp eye and outstanding editorial assistance. Our fruitful cooperation has lasted for several years and resulted in a number of successful book projects. Her kind assistance was especially valuable as neither author is a native English-speaker. Connie Wall edited the book in the last phase of the project. We appreciate the efforts of Anna Helleday, Head of the SIPRI Finance and Administration Department, who was in charge of administering the USIP grant. Cynthia Loo, SIPRI Arms Transfers Project Secretary; Dr Timothy D. Sisk, Program Officer, USIP; and April R. Hall, Grant Administrator, USIP, provided assistance in numerous ways.

We are grateful to a number of research centres and institutions—COPRI; the Institut Française des Relations Internationales (IFRI), Paris; the IISS, London; the Harrison Programme on the Future Global Agenda at the University of Maryland; the Department of Political Science, University of

Nizhniy Novgorod; the Department of Politics, School of Sociology, Politics and Anthropology, La Trobe University, Melbourne; and the Salzburg Seminar, Salzburg, which provided us with excellent research environments and warm hospitality. Without their support and assistance, this work could not have been completed.

A generous grant from the USIP made this research report possible.

Alexander A. Sergounin
Sergey V. Subbotin
University of Nizhniy Novgorod, Russia
May 1998

Acronyms

AAM	Air-to-air missile
ACDA	Arms Control and Disarmament Agency (USA)
AEW	Airborne early-warning
AFV	Armoured fighting vehicle
AIFV	Armoured infantry fighting vehicle
AMRAAM	Advanced medium-range air-to-air missile
APC	Armoured personnel carrier
APEC	Asia–Pacific Economic Cooperation forum
ARF	ASEAN Regional Forum
ASEAN	Association of South-East Asian Nations
ASEAN–PMC	ASEAN Post Ministerial Conference
ASEM	Asia–Europe Meeting
ASW	Anti-submarine warfare
ATSC	Aerospace Technology System Corporation
AWAC	Airborne warning and control
BICC	Bonn International Center for Conversion
CIA	Central Intelligence Agency (USA)
CIS	Commonwealth of Independent States
CSBM	Confidence- and security-building measure
CSCAP	Council for Security Cooperation in the Asia Pacific
CSCE	Conference on Security and Co-operation in Europe
DIA	Defense Intelligence Agency (USA)
EU	European Union
GATT	General Agreement on Tariffs and Trade
GIU	Glavnoye inzhenernoye upravleniye (Central Engineering Directorate, Russia)
GKVTP	Gosudarstvenny komitet voyenno-tekhnicheskoy politike (State Committee on Military–Technical Policy, Russia)
GNP	Gross national product
GUSK	Glavnoye upravleniye po sotrudnichestvu i kooperatsii (Central Directorate of Collaboration and Cooperation, Russia)
IAPO	Irkutsk Aircraft Production Association
ICBM	Intercontinental ballistic missile
ICV	Infantry combat vehicle
IFV	Infantry fighting vehicle
IISS	International Institute for Strategic Studies

IMF	International Monetary Fund
INS/GPS	Inertial Navigation System/Global Positioning System
KMS	Koordinatsionniy mezhvedomstvenny sovet po voenno-tekhnicheskomu sotrudnichestvu Rossiyskoy Federatsii s inostrannymi gosudarstvami (Interdepartmental Coordinating Council on Military–Technical Cooperation between the Russian Federation and Foreign States)
KMSVTP	Koordinirovanny mezhduvedomstvenny sovet po voyenno-tekhnicheskoy politike (Interdepartmental Coordinating Council for Military–Technical Policy, Russia)
KVTS	Mezhvedomstvennaya komissiya po voyenno-tekhnicheskomu sotrudnichestvu Rossiyskoy Federatsii s inostrannymi gosudarstvami (Interdepartmental Commission on Military–Technical Cooperation between the Russian Federation and Foreign Countries)
LDPR	Liberal Democratic Party of Russia
MAPO	Moscow Aircraft Production Organization
MBT	Main battle tank
MFER	Ministry of Foreign Economic Relations (Russia)
MFERC	Ministry of Foreign Economic Relations and Commerce (Russia)
MIRV	Multiple independently targetable re-entry vehicle
MLU	Mid-life upgrade
MOD	Ministry of Defence (Russia)
MTCR	Missile Technology Control Regime
NATO	North Atlantic Treaty Organization
NPT	Non-Proliferation Treaty
OSCE	Organization for Security and Co-operation in Europe
PLA	People's Liberation Army (China)
PLAAF	People's Liberation Army Air Force (China)
PLAN	People's Liberation Army Navy (China)
R&D	Research and development
SAM	Surface-to-air missile
SSBN	Nuclear-powered ballistic-missile submarine
SSM	Surface-to surface missile
SVR	Sluzhba Vneshney Razvedki (Foreign Intelligence Service, Russia)
UNIDIR	United Nations Institute for Disarmament Research
V/STOL	Vertical and short take-off and landing
WTO	Warsaw Treaty Organization

Conventions in tables

. .	Data not available or not applicable
( )	Uncertain data
b.	Billion
m.	Million
$	US dollars

1. Introduction

I. Russian policy towards East Asia

The East Asia region[1] is of vital and growing concern to Russia. Russia is interested in development of the Russian far east—itself a part of East Asia—through cooperation with the neighbouring countries. East Asia is an extremely important market for Russian military and other products. In the 1990s Russia has sold arms to the East Asian countries for as much as $1 billion a year.[2]

The Pacific Rim countries are also at the forefront of a major change in global power: with the end of the cold war, the focus is shifting from the military to the economic aspects of power. The Asia–Pacific region[3] is the world's largest consumer market, accounting for over one-third of total world trade and half the world gross national product (GNP).[4]

East Asia also has enormous strategic significance. It is still an area of immense concentration of military power, with many of the largest armies in the world, and a number of unsettled territorial and ethno-religious conflicts are causing or could cause instability in the region. Russia is a party to some of these disputes.

Five centres of power interact in the region: the Association of South-East Asian Nations (ASEAN),[5] China, Japan, Russia and the United States. With the collapse of the USSR, the end of the cold war and the growth of local economic powers, the regional balance changed dramatically. However, it is still unclear what the outcome of this process, influenced both by regional and global dynamics, will be.

Given the power shifts in the region as well as in Europe, Russia is trying to redefine its security strategy in such a way as to find counter-

---

[1] East Asia is defined for the purposes of this book as consisting of Brunei, Cambodia, China, Indonesia, Japan, North Korea, South Korea, Laos, Malaysia, Mongolia, Myanmar, the Philippines, Singapore, Taiwan, Thailand and Viet Nam.

[2] *Izvestiya,* 22 Sep. 1994, p. 3, and 15 Mar. 1997, p. 4.

[3] Asia–Pacific is defined for the purposes of this book as consisting of the East Asian countries plus Australia, Canada, New Zealand and the USA.

[4] Lasater, M., *The New Pacific Community: US Strategic Options in Asia* (Westview Press: Boulder, Colo., 1996), p. ix.

[5] ASEAN was established by the Bangkok Declaration of 1967. As of 1998, Brunei, Indonesia, Laos, Malaysia, Myanmar, the Philippines, Singapore, Thailand and Viet Nam were members. Cambodia had expected to join in July 1997 but its admission was put off because of the political situation there.

balances to both the local resurgent powers and the enlargement of the North Atlantic Treaty Organization (NATO) and the European Union (EU). For these reasons, the Russian leadership regards the East Asian dimension of its foreign policy as critical to the success of its post-cold war strategy. Russia needs an effective strategy towards the region to serve its economic, security, political and cultural interests.

The main problem for Russia with regard to the region is staying engaged and remaining an important player in the future development of the Asia–Pacific region. This has been made difficult for two reasons. First, Russian military power has been dramatically reduced in the region. Russia can no longer afford to maintain the same level of military presence there as the Soviet Union did. Second, economic strength has become the most important manifestation of a country's power and significance, and because of the dire economic conditions that now prevail in Russia it currently does not have much to offer the countries of East Asia.

Despite its economic and military weakness, Russia is trying to conduct an active policy in the area on both the multilateral and bilateral levels. Its arms sales policy is the most dynamic dimension of its security strategy in the region. With arms exports, Russia hopes to compensate for its lack of economic and diplomatic instruments as well as to support the Russian defence industry.

Surprisingly, over several years Russia has managed to re-establish its defence ties not only with former Soviet clients such as Laos, Myanmar (formerly Burma) and Viet Nam but also with China, which Soviet strategists regarded as the second-greatest enemy after the United States. Russia has also succeeded in penetrating new arms markets such as the member states of ASEAN and South Korea, which were closed to Russia for ideological reasons and because of Western domination.

These developments have attracted a great deal of attention from the world research community. This study seeks to broaden the understanding of Russia's post-communist arms transfer policies in East Asia by considering the following three fundamental questions:

1. What are the domestic and international determinants of Russia's arms trade strategy in the area?
2. How do the Russian arms export decision-making and management systems operate?

3. What are the actual programmes of military–technical cooperation between Russia and the East Asian countries?

In addressing these questions, this book shows that Russia's arms transfer policy is not a separate or isolated segment of its international strategy by examining arms sales in the general context of Russian domestic and foreign policy. Arms trade policy is both a product of the national debate and an instrument of Russia's foreign policy in the region.

II. The research agenda

The three questions posed in section I form the core of a broad research agenda which consists of a number of vexed and under-researched problems.

First, the question arises why Russia has become so aggressive on the world's arms markets generally and in particular in East Asia. This provokes further questions. Why has it abandoned the policy of arms export restraint held by the USSR during the latter part of the administration of President Mikhail Gorbachev and by Russia in the early years of President Boris Yeltsin's presidency? Did Russia launch an expansion of its arms sales because of domestic economic difficulties or to counteract the Western lack of restraint in the arms trade? Or was arms trade policy the only effective security policy tool available to Russia in this situation and these other considerations relatively unimportant?

The research literature on arms transfers often stresses that economic benefits—such as a more favourable balance of payments, lower unemployment, reductions in weapon unit costs, increased turnover and profit, and avoidance of interruptions in arms design and production work—and some strategic considerations—such as the need for friends and allies and the hope of gaining more influence in certain regions—are powerful incentives for arms exports. However, the extent to which these factors have affected Russia's motivation remains unclear. Some reports suggest that proceeds from arms sales have helped Russia in making its defence industry or at least some of its sectors economically viable. Other accounts would have it that the Russian leadership is not interested in supporting the defence industry but in obtaining revenue for conversion of the arms industry to civilian production and overall restructuring of the former Soviet highly militarized economy. An explanation of the arms trade as a dirty but profitable business which serves the group interests of some clans within the military, economic and political elites is also popular among Russian journalists and the general public.

Similarly, there are many different interpretations of Russia's foreign policy and strategic motives. If arms transfers are an effective instrument for ensuring a country's security and international standing, why is Russia providing China, a candidate for regional leadership, with advanced weaponry? It is obvious that under certain circumstances China's new military capabilities could be used against Russia. Is not this military–technical cooperation detrimental to Russia's long-term national interests? Answers to these questions vary depending not only on the degree of the observer's optimism or pessimism but also on his or her political and ideological sympathies and theoretical underpinnings.

There are also grounds for asking whether there are any strategic considerations behind Russia's arms transfer policies towards East Asia. Are domestic economic and political rationales dominant? If they are not, why is Russia supplying arms to China, South Korea, Malaysia and Viet Nam when there are active confrontations or competition between them? (There have been reports that Russia is prepared to resume arms transfers to North Korea and even sell weapons to Taiwan.) It is difficult to understand what political and strategic ends such an arms export policy serves. Can it really help Russia to acquire new friends, contain any country seeking regional hegemony or resolve any local conflict?

The second basic question considered in this study—how decisions on Russian arms transfers are made and implemented—has also not been thoroughly explored. However, it should be noted that the lack of reliable public sources limits the scope for analysis in this field. Moreover, arms regulations and the decision-making system for arms transfers are extremely unstable in post-communist Russia. Arms export legislation and key actors change so fast that it is difficult to define the core and the periphery of decision making, the actors in the arms trade business, the ground rules, and so on.[6]

---

[6] For descriptions of the decision-making process, see chapter 3 in this volume; and Litavrin, P., 'The process of policy making and licensing for conventional arms transfers', ed. I. Anthony, SIPRI, *Russia and the Arms Trade* (Oxford University Press: Oxford, 1998), pp. 107–16.

The study of the Russian decision-making system not only provides analysts with knowledge of the behind-the-scenes process but also encourages them to question why democratization of the system has not been completed. Why is there still no effective parliamentary control over arms transfer policy? Why has the government, in fact, returned to Soviet-style centralized practices in arms export? Why are many arms producers dissatisfied with existing arms export procedures? In addressing these questions, the student of Russian arms transfer policy has to link this problem to the broader context of Russian domestic politics and highlight the difficulties in creating an effective foreign policy decision-making mechanism in a period of transition.

This book also sheds light on the nature of the supplier–recipient relationship in the case of Russian arms transfers to East Asia. In the past, Soviet arms transfers were politically and ideologically motivated and serious attention was not paid to the economic dimensions of military–technical cooperation with foreign countries. Many arms and technology transfer programmes were conducted on a grant basis. The USSR's relations with recipients were, moreover, mainly of the patron–client type, which implied a certain degree of control by the supplier over the recipient's foreign policy behaviour.[7]

In the post-cold war era the very nature of Russian arms transfer policy has changed. Now commercial rather than strategic or ideological considerations dominate Russian arms sales. Russia became dissatisfied with its partners, who tended to prefer a barter form of payment, and insisted on a larger element of hard currency. At the same time it was unable to retain the patron–client pattern of relations with the East Asian countries. Russia did not even attempt to exert influence on the recipients because it was afraid of a hostile reaction. In addition, its partners have diversified their sources of arms imports in order to avoid over-dependence on one supplier. At the most Russia has been able to exert only indirect influence through arms transfers.

Military–technical cooperation helps to create a certain interdependence, which has a harmonizing effect on supplier–recipient relations and facilitates the search for common approaches to regional problems. However, interdependence means that not only the recipient but also the supplier becomes dependent on its partner. Chinese,

[7] Kirshin, Yu., 'Conventional arms transfers during the Soviet period', ed. Anthony (note 7), pp. 38–70.

Malaysian and South Korean orders were critical for Russia's troubled defence economy and Russia did not want to lose them. In the case of South Korea, Russia had to repay its debts by arms transfers. Russia was also dependent on the trade in arms with China in the sense that it could improve bilateral relations and redirect China's attention from the north to the south and south-east.

The security implications of Russian arms transfers to East Asia are another vexed question in the research literature and public debates. If it is true that Russian arms sales are mainly driven by economic considerations, can Russia be a responsible arms supplier? Is Russia able to avoid destabilizing arms transfers or not?

Moreover, it is impossible to study Russian arms export policy without taking into account other suppliers' practices, as they also shape the East Asian security environment. Russian policy is only one, and not the most powerful, input among many. It is useful to study how Russia interacts with other regional and global actors rather than to treat it as an autonomous player. The same is true where the prospects for arms control and restraint in East Asia are concerned. In this regard, it is not helpful to concentrate on measures taken unilaterally by Russia. There are many reasons to believe that only multilateral arrangements can neutralize the negative effects of the arms trade in the region and contribute to the creation of a more stable and secure environment in East Asia.

III. Sources

The publications of international organizations (e.g., the UN and its bodies, ASEAN and the EU) were important sources in the research for this book. UN materials on arms transfers and arms control developments in East Asia include the reports on the UN Register of Conventional Arms, published annually, UN yearbooks and bulletins which include reports on the UN General Assembly, Security Council and Committee on Disarmament sessions and resolutions, and publications of the United Nations Institute for Disarmament Research (UNIDIR).

Of the national government publications and official documents, Russian official documents are of particular interest and importance. There are several categories: (*a*) presidential and prime ministerial decrees and other documents; (*b*) publications of certain government agencies involved in Asia–Pacific policy, such as the Ministry of Foreign Affairs, the Ministry of Defence, the Ministry of Foreign Economic Relations and the State Committee on Military–Technical Policy; and (c) documents of the State Duma, the lower house of the Russian Parliament.[8] The Russian Government has declassified some general data on the Russian military posture, arms transfers and military assistance to the East Asian countries but refused to provide details on particular countries and programmes. Russia also does not disclose the categories of arms and military services or figures on orders and actual deliveries.

Because of the lack of Russian official statistics, the official publications of other countries are important, particularly those of the USA. They provide information and statistics both on the legislative basis of Russia's arms transfer policy and on details of particular programmes. Of the US congressional publications, committee hearings and reports, the *Congressional Record* and reports of the Congressional Research Service of the Library of Congress are invaluable sources. Of the publications of the US executive branch, those of the Arms Control and Disarmament Agency (ACDA) on world military expenditure and arms transfers and those of the Departments of State, Defense and Commerce are valuable. In addition to analysis of Russian security policies in the region, these sources depict the entire strategic context of the East Asian region and the policies of the major regional and global players. Some information on arms transfers in the region can be found in Australian, Chinese, Japanese, Taiwanese and other official publications, mostly in White Papers. However, compared to Russian and US publications they contain little information on particular Russian arms transfers.

The SIPRI arms transfers database is unique and covers both orders and deliveries of major conventional weapons, regional dynamics and worldwide trends. A complete register of Russian transfers to countries in East Asia in the period 1992–98 is presented in the appendix to this volume.

---

[8] The official bulletin *Sobraniye Zakonodatelstva Rossiyskoy Federatsii* (Collection of Legislative Acts of the Russian Federation) publishes reports on the State Duma debates and foreign policy platforms of the political parties and *Mezhdunarodnaya Zhizn* has published interviews with Duma leaders, but the authors have mainly used committee and party background material such as drafts of legislative acts, statements and declarations. This category of documents was formerly circulated as unpublished manuscripts or memoranda. They have been valuable for examination of the Russian foreign policy schools of thought and the Duma's role in the shaping of arms transfer policy.

Monographs, articles and scholarly works on Russian policy and international security in the region are cited extensively in this book.

Research papers on security politics in the Asia–Pacific region are published by various US, regional, European and Russian research institutes, such as Aarhus University, Denmark; the Bonn International Center for Conversion (BICC); the Center for Strategic and International Studies, Washington, DC; the China Institute of International Studies, Beijing; the Chinese Council of Advanced Policy Studies, Taipei; the Institute for Defense Studies and Analyses, New Delhi; the Institute for Far Eastern Studies, Moscow; the Institute of International Relations, Taipei; the Institute of Southeast Asian Studies, Singapore; the International Institute for Strategic Studies, London (IISS); the Program in Arms Control, Disarmament, and International Security, University of Illinois, Urbana–Champaign; RAND, Santa Monica, California; SIPRI; the Strategic Studies Institute, US Army War College, Carlisle Barracks, Pennsylvania; the Sun Yat-Sen Center for Policy Studies, Kaohsiung, Taiwan; and others.

Annual reference works such as the *SIPRI Yearbook: Armaments, Disarmament and International Security; The Military Balance* and *Strategic Survey* (IISS); *Asian Security* (Research Institute for Peace and Security, Tokyo); and *World Defence Almanac* (published as the first issue each year of the journal *Military Technology*) were useful primarily because they provide consistent coverage over long periods of time. Several major Russian, Asian and Western newspapers, journals and bulletin publications were also used extensively.

As with any study of arms transfer policies, it is difficult to compile a set of reliable data. There are some newspaper and journal interviews with Chinese and Russian officials and the two countries' reports to the UN Register of Conventional Arms but, as noted above, few official sources are available. Bilateral agreements on military–technical cooperation and detailed information on arms and technology transfers and defence industry cooperation are usually classified or not fully reported. The scholar must examine numerous unconfirmed reports in the mass media to select data. Research is also complicated by differences of opinion between experts as regards methods of assessment of statistics related to arms transfers. Moreover, research techniques and terminology vary. The exercise of judgement and careful comparisons between sources have therefore been important elements in the compilation of data for this study.

There are three general criteria for the selection of sources. The first is representativeness: the data should represent the main trends in Russian arms transfer policy in the region. The second is the identity of the source: the author and historical and ideological (if any) background should be identified. The third concerns originality and informativeness: sources which provide new information or new approaches are of paramount interest.

It was important to use an appropriate method of measuring and evaluating the arms trade. The authors use the widely recognized SIPRI method—a trend-indicator device designed to measure changes in the flow of major conventional weapons and its geographic pattern. These values are expressed in monetary terms, reflecting both the quantity and the quality of the weapons transferred. They do not correspond to the actual prices paid. Aggregate values are based only on actual deliveries during the years covered in this study.[9]

These techniques help to overcome the limitations of the sources and compile substantial and sufficient data for the study.

IV. Structure of the book

The questions listed in section I of this chapter determined the structure of the book.

Chapter 2 examines the determinants of Russian military–technical cooperation with the East Asian countries and analyses the domestic economic, social, political and security factors shaping Russia's arms transfer policies. It also describes the current Russian security debate and different schools of thought in foreign policy and the international environment—the global and regional security dynamics and power shifts and Russia's bilateral relations with East Asian countries.

Chapter 3 describes the Russian arms transfer decision-making system. It presents data on Russia's export regulations, the evolution of the government structures charged with responsibility for arms transfers, the management of production, the relationship between the government and the defence industry, the administrative and financial

[9] For further detail, see 'Sources and methods', *SIPRI Yearbook 1998: Armaments, Disarmament and International Security* (Oxford University Press: Oxford, 1998), appendix 8C, pp. 369–70. The full description of the methodology is available on the SIPRI Internet site, URL <http://www.sipri.se/projects/armstrade/atmethods.html>. It is important to note that other figures for the value of particular arms transfers, orders or deals cited in this book should not be compared with the SIPRI trend-indicator values.

dimensions of arms sales, and so on. It ends with an analysis of the major problems confronting the decision-making system.

Chapter 4 reviews the major programmes of Sino-Russian military cooperation in the 1990s. It presents data on acquisitions of Russian weapon systems and military technology by the Chinese land forces, Air Force and Navy and examines the influence of arms imports on China's defence modernization programmes and military potential. The chapter also depicts Sino-Russian defence industry, military-to-military and intelligence cooperation and concludes that Russian arms transfers have become an important part of China's military modernization programme and could lead to a significant increase in China's military capabilities. However, Sino-Russian military cooperation should not be overestimated because it is driven mainly by economic interests, the two countries have not yet resolved many bilateral problems, Russia fears Chinese hegemonism in the future, and China is opting for diversification of its arms import sources in order to avoid over-dependence on Russia.

Chapter 5 examines Russia's arms transfer policies towards the ASEAN states, some of which represent fairly new markets for Russia. Russia has not only successfully entered new markets but also restored, although on a new basis, military relations with former clients of the USSR. The incentives and future prospects for military cooperation between Russia and the South-East Asian countries are also considered.

Chapter 6 addresses Russia's arms transfer policies towards the Korean peninsula. The collapse of world socialism and the rapprochement between Russia and South Korea have destroyed the former basis for intensive Russian military–technical cooperation with North Korea. Nevertheless, Russia and North Korea hope to rebuild their relations in the defence field on new premises. Reports of the mass migration of Russian scientists specializing in weapons of mass destruction to North Korea are evaluated. The motivation for, historical background to and patterns of Russian–South Korean military–technical cooperation are examined. The chapter concludes that Russia still lacks a coherent and sound arms sale strategy towards the two Korean states.

Chapter 7 assesses the security implications of Russian arms and military technology transfers to the region and presents a number of conclusions. It examines the ways in which these transfers have affected Russia's bilateral relations with recipients and its regional and global security relations. The chapter identifies the positive and negative consequences of Russian arms sales policies in East Asia. On the one hand, defence cooperation has had a clearly positive effect on Russia's bilateral relations; on the other hand, Russian arms trade policy has a mixed record as regards its impact on the regional and global security systems. In particular, many regional and global actors are worried about Sino-Russian military rapprochement because it could contribute to the rise of China as a dominant regional power, stimulate regional tensions and arms competition, and lead to the forging of a new, powerful strategic alliance between China and Russia.

2. The determinants of Russian arms trade policy

I. Introduction

The issue of the motivation of arms suppliers has received much attention from the research community.[1] The concept of supply and demand factors, both domestic and international, is commonly used in the literature. The major supply factors include: (*a*) the economic interest of arms-producing companies in profits, economies of scale, the recouping of research and development (R&D) costs, and employment; (*b*) the interest of the governments of supplier states in maintaining a viable base of arms production and technology, employment and tax revenues; and (*c*) the interest of governments in supporting allied or friendly states by increasing their military capabilities and acquiring some measure of influence over recipient governments.[2]

This conceptual framework is helpful in analysing Russia's motivations. Two main factors shape Russian arms transfer policy towards East Asia: (*a*) the domestic environment (e.g., the military–industrial complex, economic adjustment, interest group politics and the ambitions of regional elites); and (*b*) the international environment (e.g., strategic and diplomatic concerns, bilateral relations and alliance politics). Russian and foreign experts differ as to which of these is the main driving force. One group of analysts views domestic (especially economic) determinants as the main motivation,[3] while other experts

---

[1] See, e.g., Brzoska, M. and Ohlson, T., SIPRI, *Arms Transfers to the Third World, 1971–85* (Oxford University Press: Oxford, 1987), pp. 125–27; Kolodziej, E., 'Arms transfers and international politics: the interdependence of independence', eds S. G. Neuman and R. E. Harkavy, *Arms Transfers in the Modern World* (Praeger: New York, 1980); Krause, K., *Arms and the State: Patterns of Military Production and Trade* (Cambridge University Press: Cambridge, 1992); and Pierre, A. J., *The Global Politics of Arms Sales* (Princeton University Press: Princeton, N.J., 1982), pp. 14–27.

[2] Catrina, C., 'Main directions of research in the arms trade', eds R. E. Harkavy and S. G. Neuman, *The Arms Trade: Problems and Prospects in the Post-Cold War World,* Special Issue of *Annals of the American Academy of Political and Social Science*, Sep. 1994, p. 196; and Catrina, C., 'Supplier policies and recipient dependence', UN, *Transparency in International Arms Transfers,* Disarmament Topical Papers no. 3 (UN: New York, 1990), p. 31.

[3] Beaver, P., 'Russian industry feels the cold', *Jane's Defence Weekly,* 7 May 1994, p. 30; Kogan, E., 'The Russian defence industry: trends, difficulties and obstacles', *Asian Defence Journal*, Oct. 1994, pp. 43–44; Kotelkin, A., 'Russia and the world arms market', *International Affairs* (Moscow), vol. 42, no. 4 (1996), pp. 33–35; Trush, S., 'Prodazha rossiyskogo

regard arms transfers as one of the most important tools of Russia's foreign and security policy in the region and see strategic interests as taking priority over economic rationales in Russia's arms trade policy.[4] A third, minor, group of analysts believe that a combination of domestic and international factors determines Russia's policy in different ways in individual cases.[5] This approach seems to offer a more appropriate concept upon which to base the analysis of Russia's decision-making system and motivation.

II. The domestic environment

The Russian defence industry

The first and most obvious rationale for Russia's arms trade policy is to provide financial support to the defence industry. Since the time of perestroika and the breakup of the Soviet Union, the formidable former Soviet military industry has found itself in deep economic decline. This dramatic development has raised some concern in the West. In December 1991 Robert Gates, then Director of the US Central Intelligence Agency (CIA), warned that

the former Soviet defence industries, enterprises involved in special weapons and missile programmes that face cuts in military funding may well try to stay in business by selling equipment, materials and services in the international market place. The hunger for hard currency could take precedence over proliferation concerns, particularly among republic and local governments with high concentrations of defence industry and little else that is marketable.[6]

oruzhiya Pekinu: rezony i opaseniya' [Russian arms sales to Beijing: pro and con], *Nezavisimaya Gazeta,* 25 Apr. 1996; and Trenin, D., 'Kak prikryt vostochny geostrategicheskiy 'fasad' Rossii?' [How to protect the eastern geo-strategic façade of Russia?], *Nezavisimoye Voyennoye Obozreniye,* no. 17 (1997), p. 4.

[4] Ching, F., 'Russia wants bigger Asian role', *Far Eastern Economic Review,* 14 Mar. 1996, p. 32; and Singh, A. I., 'India's relations with Russia and Central Asia', *International Affairs* (London), vol. 71, no. 1 (1995), p. 71.

[5] Blank, S. J., *Challenging the New World Order: The Arms Transfers Policies of the Russian Republic* (Strategic Studies Institute, US Army War College: Carlisle Barracks, Pa., 1993), pp. 43–44; and Hickey, D. V. and Harmel, C. C., 'United States and China's military ties with the Russian republics', *Asian Affairs,* vol. 20, no. 4 (winter 1994), p. 244.

[6] US Congress, House of Representatives, Committee on Armed Services, *Potential Threats to American Security in the Post-Cold War Era,* Hearings before the Defense Policy Panel of the Committee on Armed Services, 102nd Congress, 1st session, 10, 11, 12 Dec. 1991 (US Government Printing Office: Washington, DC, 1992), p. 9.

Table 2.1. Indicators of economic decline in the Russian defence industries, 1991–94[a]

Industry	Total output			Employment			Salaries	
	1992 as % of 1991	1993 as % of 1992	1994 as % of 1993	1992 as % of 1991	1993 as % of 1992	1994 as % of 1993	1992 as % of industry average	1993 as % of industry average
Aircraft	84	81	(49)	91	90	(85)	71	68
Ammunition and special chemicals	70	82	(62)	90	89	(81)	71	63
Armaments	84	82	(54)	93	91	(85)	68	64
Atomic industry	100	103	(77)	97	97	(94)	114	119
Communications equipment	74	78	(55)	87	82	(82)	56	51
Electronics	72	66	(49)	92	81	(76)	54	44
Radio	84	93	(55)	87	86	(82)	53	53
Shipbuilding	89	88	(76)	90	90	(86)	77	87
Space	94	95	(71)	89	89	(82)	66	69
Total defence complex	**82**	**84**	**(65)**	**91**	**88**	**(84)**	**69**	**67**

[a] Includes civilian and military production in the defence complex.

Source: Sköns, E. and Gonchar, Ks., 'Arms production', *SIPRI Yearbook 1995: Armaments, Disarmament and International Security* (Oxford University Press: Oxford, 1995), table 13.9, p. 473.

Gates' fears were well founded. In 1993 the CIA reported that 'Russia has been actively promoting military sales to China this year to secure needed hard currency and to help defence industries cope with declines in domestic procurement'.[7]

The Russian leadership has often stressed the need to keep production facilities, technicians and scientists employed lest massive unemployment and falling investment ruin the sector and undermine readiness and technological competitiveness. In 1992 alone, military procurement was cut by 70 per cent.[8] According to estimates of the Moscow-based economics agency Novecon, defence production fell by 33.4 per cent in 1993.[9] The situation has not improved since then. By the end of 1994 about 400 defence enterprises had stopped all production, while another 1500 were working part-time.[10] In 1994 Russia had 1900 defence plants—by 1997 the number had fallen to 1760 and, according to former Minister of the Economy Yakov Urinson, by 2000 it will drop to 700 and by 2005 to 500.[11]

Output in the defence sector fell by 39.6 per cent and the number of employees by 13.6 per cent during 1996.[12] In 1997 military output was 70.7 per cent of what it had been in 1996.[13] The Ministry of the Economy estimated that 2.5 million employees out of 6.1 million left the defence industry in the five years 1991–95.[14] According to the League of Assistance to Defence Enterprises, the leading lobbying organization of the Russian military–industrial complex, only 10 per cent of the industry's capacity was being used in 1996.[15] Table 2.1 illustrates the economic decline of the Russian defence industry in 1992–94.

As the Secretary of the Security Council's Komissiya Soveta Bezopasnosti po Oboronnoy Promyshlennosti (Commission on the

[7] Nai-kuo, H., 'Russia promoting military sales to mainland China', Central News Agency (Taipei), 12 Oct. 1993; and Hickey and Harmel (note 5), p. 244.

[8] Bonn International Center for Conversion, *Chancen und Probleme der Rustungskonversion in der GUS* [The prospects and problems of conversion in the CIS] (BICC: Bonn, 1995), p. 4.

[9] Beaver (note 3), p. 30.

[10] *Segodnya*, 18 Oct. 1994, p. 3.

[11] Karatov, Y., 'Government hopes to bring arms exports to $5 billion in 1998', Russian Information Agency (RIA) Novosti, *Daily Review*, 23 Jan. 1998, issue 002.

[12] *Krasnaya Zvezda*, 3 Aug. 1996, p. 3.

[13] Maslyukov Y., 'Voenno-promyshlenny kompleks nuzhdaetsya v pomoshchi' [The military–industrial complex needs help], *Nezavisimaya Gazeta*, 17 Jan. 1998, p. 3.

[14] Hull, A. and Markov, D., 'A changing market in the arms bazaar', *Jane's Intelligence Review*, Mar. 1997, p. 140.

[15] Pappe, Y., 'Otraslevye lobbi v pravitelstve Rossii' [Sectorial lobbies in the Russian Government], *Pro et Contra*, autumn 1996, p. 69; and *Rossiyskaya Gazeta*, 28 Apr. 1997, p. 1.

Defence Industry) stated, cuts in arms procurement and R&D funds in 1991–95 led to the ending of the production of 175 different types of arms. The General Staff of the Russian Armed Forces estimated in 1995 that, if current practices continued, only 10 per cent of the equipment of the Russian military would be modern weapons by the year 2000.[16]

The Russian Government has often been unable to pay the defence industry for weapons ordered. In 1993 over 100 new MiG-29 fighter aircraft worth $2 billion were parked, unclaimed and unpaid for, at a MiG assembly plant near Moscow.[17] In 1994–95 the MOD paid for only 23 per cent of an order placed with the Fakel (Torch) enterprise, builder of air-defence missile systems.[18] The government owed the Nizhniy Novgorod defence industry 150 billion roubles by the end of 1994.[19] According to Viktor Glukhikh, at that time Chairman of the Gosudarstvenny Komitet Oboronnoy Promyshlennosti (Goskom-oboronprom, the State Committee on Defence Industries), by the end of 1993 the government owed the defence industry 8 trillion roubles.[20] Unpaid government debts stood at 11 trillion roubles at the end of 1995 and at 18.5 trillion roubles at the beginning of 1998.[21]

Among other negative consequences, government non-payment of debts has prevented the defence industry from pursuing an effective arms export policy because plants have no money to start production of equipment ordered by foreign clients.

The Russian leadership turned to arms exports in the hope of saving the slowly dying defence industry. As President Yeltsin noted, 'the weapons trade is essential for us to obtain the foreign currency which we urgently need and to keep the defence industry afloat'.[22]

As an illustration of how military exports can be helpful in this regard, it may be noted that in 1993 the Russian defence industry repaid 400 billion roubles ($220 million) in loan credits from Russian

---

[16] *Nezavisimaya Gazeta,* 15 Apr. 1995, p. 3; and Khripunov, I., 'Conventional weapons transfers: US–Russian cooperation or rivalry', *Comparative Strategy,* vol. 14 (1995), p. 456.

[17] Kogan (note 3), pp. 43–44.

[18] *Izvestiya,* 10 Oct. 1995, p. 4.

[19] *Izvestiya,* 10 Oct. 1995, p. 5, in Foreign Broadcast Information Service, *Daily Report– Central Eurasia (FBIS-SOV),* FBIS-SOV-95-205-S, 24 Oct. 1995, pp. 33–37.

[20] *Komsomolskaya Pravda,* 27 Apr. 1994, p. 2.

[21] Menon, R., 'The strategic convergence between Russia and China', *Survival,* vol. 39, no. 2 (summer 1997), p. 110; and *Rossiyskaya Gazeta,* 8 Apr. 1998, p. 1.

[22] *Izvestiya,* 22 Feb. 1992, p. 4. See also Yeltsin, B., 'The basic provisions of the military doctrine of the Russian Federation', *Jane's Intelligence Review, Special Report,* Jan. 1994, p. 12.

state and commercial banks from its profits from export orders.[23] Over 50 per cent of arms production is funded by proceeds from arms exports, according to Alexander Kotelkin, former Director General of the state arms trade company Rosvooruzheniye.[24] The production of some weapon systems depends entirely on foreign orders. For example, the MiG-29 fighter aircraft has not been produced for the Russian Air Force for six years. In the period 1993–97, MiG-MAPO (the Moscow Aircraft Production Organization) sold 28 aircraft to Hungary, 18 to Malaysia, 13 to Slovakia, 10 to India, 5 to Romania and 1 to Iran; 40 MiG-29s were to have been produced in 1997.[25]

Taking into account the lack of state orders and funding, the proceeds from arms exports are crucial if the defence industry is to develop new weapon systems. According to Anatoliy Belosvet, First Deputy Director of MiG-MAPO, the $22 million which the company would earn from the sale of MiG-29s to Malaysia would pay for the construction of the MiG-37, the Russian version of a stealth fighter.[26] According to Kotelkin, in 1995 alone Rosvooruzheniye invested over $400 million in the Russian military–industrial complex, of which about 50 per cent was from its own funds.[27] Deputy Director Vladimir Vypryazhkin has said that Rosvooruzheniye invested over $600 million in the defence industry in 1996.[28]

Russian officials claim that the opening or restoration of military ties with some East Asian countries is the natural outgrowth of broad and maturing relationships with them. It appears, however, that economic concerns are the driving force behind Russia's decision to intensify its arms sales policy towards the region. Igor Rogachev, Russian Ambassador to China, explained: 'I think it's quite natural that we consider this [military] cooperation as an integral part of our general relationship. China has been and I hope it will be our partner. Our defence industry needs some impulse. We need hard currency. We now have a lot of economic troubles'.[29] In 1996 the Russian

---

[23] Beaver (note 3), p. 30.

[24] *Izvestiya,* 20 Sep. 1996, p. 4; and Pappe (note 15), p. 69.

[25] It was reported that the aircraft were for export. Butowski, P., 'Thrust-vectoring will drive MiG-29 exports', *Jane's Defence Weekly,* 21 May 1997, p. 28.

[26] *Asian Defence Journal,* Dec. 1995, p. 131. There seems to be no MiG-37 in production or development, although there is no information that its development has been stopped.

[27] Kotelkin (note 3), p. 33.

[28] Perera, J., 'Rosvooruzheniye sets 1997 targets', *Jane's Intelligence Review and Jane's Sentinel Pointer,* June 1997, p. 3.

[29] 'Russia hopes to sell more arms to Peking', Central News Agency (Taipei), 15 Dec. 1992.

deputy prime minister remarked in Malaysia that Russia is 'willing to sell anything that our customers want, except nuclear weapons'.[30]

Today Russia is willing to sell arms even to its former enemies and rivals if they are ready to pay in hard currency and to countries in conflict so long as this does not adversely affect its relations with other states. According to former Deputy Minister for Foreign Economic Relations Sergey Glaziev, in 1992 the ministry was ready to issue a licence for the sale of ships, missiles and light arms to Taiwan if the Russian leadership decided that arms transfers to Taiwan would not harm relations with mainland China.[31] Former Minister for Foreign Economic Relations Pyotr Aven noted that in 1992 Russian defence plants put formidable pressure on the government to permit arms deals with Taiwan.[32]

The need for hard currency for economic reform

Russian arms exports have been at the centre of a fundamental debate over where the resources needed to implement economic reform should come from. Some Russian politicians and industrialists claim that arms sales can finance economic reform, in particular conversion. By some accounts, Russia delivered arms worth $1.71 billion in 1994, $3.07 billion in 1995, $3.56 billion in 1996 and $2.2–2.6 billion in 1997.[33] These figures are comparable with the total amount of annual Western assistance to Russia. Additional long-term contracts were at this time also nearing completion, worth $8.5 billion up to 2003.[34] According to Oleg Sidorenko, former Deputy Director General of Rosvooruzheniye, Russia plans to match the United States' share of the market by the turn of the century.[35] Mikhail Maley, a former

[30] Hull and Markov (note 14), pp. 140–41.

[31] *Rossiyskaya Gazeta,* 4 Mar. 1992, p. 3.

[32] *Izvestiya,* 14 Mar. 1992, p. 4.

[33] Rybas, A., 'Opasnaya tendentsiya' [Dangerous tendency], *Nezavisimoye Voyennoye Obozreniye*, 12–19 Feb. 1998, p. 6. According to Boris N. Kuzyk, former assistant to the president on military–technical cooperation, Russia concluded contracts worth $2.5 billion and delivered arms worth $3.05 billion in 1995. *Rossiyskaya Gazeta,* 17 Oct. 1995, p. 3; and *Nezavisimaya Gazeta,* 25 Apr. 1996, p. 2. Kotelkin and Sidorenko of Rosvooruzheniye said that Russian arms exports reached $3.5–3.6 billion in 1996. Kotelkin (note 3), p. 38; and Perera, J., 'Russia's arms sales increasing', *Jane's Intelligence Review and Jane's Sentinel Pointer*, Jan. 1997, p. 2.

[34] Klenov, V., 'Slukhi o smerti "oboronki", pokhozhe, silno preuvelicheny' [It appears that rumours of the defence industry's death are strongly exaggerated], *Rossiyskaya Gazeta*, 30 Apr. 1998, p. 10.

[35] Perera (note 28), p. 3.

adviser to Yeltsin, has suggested that Russia must sell $5–10 billion worth of arms annually for 15–30 years to cover the $150 billion estimated cost of conversion.[36] Many Russian analysts have pointed out, however, that the state conversion programmes started in 1993 were completely destroyed by the unwise policy of the government itself and the general economic crisis. The proceeds from arms sales disappeared into the 'black hole' of the troubled Russian economy.[37]

No reliable and complete data on Russia's profits from arms exports are available. According to Aleksei Ogarev, deputy chief of the president's staff, and journalist Pavel Felgengauer, $2.13 billion in hard currency and $354 million in clearing currencies were transferred to the Rosvooruzheniye accounts in 1996. These figures do not include the value of weapons delivered by Russia to foreign countries to repay its foreign debts.[38]

The influence of social factors

Between 1991 and 1997, Russia's military–industrial complex lost 2.5 million workers, bringing the industry's workforce down to 3.6 million employees.[39] In early 1995 the Russian Defence Industry Workers' Union urged its members to prepare for action aimed at forcing the resignation of the government and the president. The union reported that workers were owed more than 160 billion roubles in back pay, while their average wage was only 62.5 per cent of the average industrial wage. It also charged that less than 30 per cent of the necessary funds was provided in 1994 for programmes to convert defence plants to civilian production.[40] This critical response from a major section of Russia's workforce (traditionally supporters of Yeltsin's reformist government) caused the Kremlin some concern in view of the parliamentary and presidential elections due in December 1995 and June 1996, respectively.

[36] *Asian Defence Journal*, no. 3 (1994), p. 74.

[37] Cooper, J., *The Soviet Defence Industry: Conversion and Economic Reforms* (Royal Institute of International Affairs/Council on Foreign Relations Press: New York, 1991), pp. 65–66; and Avduevsky, V., 'Conversion and economic reforms: experience of Russia', *Peace and the Sciences*, Mar. 1992, pp. 7–10.

[38] 'Russia as an arms dealer', Interview with Aleksei Ogarev, Russian Information Agency (RIA) Novosti, *Daily Review*, 6 Jan. 1998, issue 001; and Felgengauer, P., 'Torgovlya oruzhiem ne tak uzh i pribylna' [Arms trade not so profitable], *Segodnya*, 26 Dec. 1997, p. 2.

[39] Hull and Markov (note 14), p. 140; and Khripunov (note 16), pp. 456–57.

[40] Khripunov (note 16), p. 457.

Arms exports have a positive effect on employment and on relations between labour and industrialists. In September 1994 a deal with China on the export of submarines prevented the financial collapse of the factory and a strike in the Krasnoye Sormovo plant in Nizhniy Novgorod.[41] Kotelkin said that the boost in arms sales in 1995–96 preserved 835 000 jobs in the industry.[42] By 2000 this figure may increase to 1.2–1.4 million.[43]

If arms transfer deals with many developing countries cannot be paid for on a purely cash basis, Russia believes that this kind of military cooperation could still contribute to resolving the problem of its consumer goods deficit. China can offer Russia a range of goods such as toys, some electronics, textiles, shoes, leather and tea. Despite the relatively low quality of Chinese goods, China is adapting to the Russian market much better than some developing and even developed countries.

Regionalism

Russian experts believe that cooperation with East Asian countries could help in development of the Russian far east.[44] This distant and underdeveloped region, with its many economic and social problems, possesses vast resources and a skilled labour force and for these reasons could be of great interest for foreign investors. Some of the defence plants producing military hardware for export to East Asia (e.g., the Gagarin Aviation Plant in Komsomolsk-na-Amure, the builder of the Su-27 fighter aircraft) are also located in the far eastern areas and thus close to their markets. Most of the defence plants involved in Sino-Russian joint projects come from Russia's Ural and Siberian regions and China's Manchuria province.[45]

Despite the economic, infrastructural and logistical problems, the emerging business community of the Russian far east, a larger Russian private sector and state-owned enterprises are entering the

[41] *Delo*, 24–30 Mar. 1995, p. 3, and 7–13 Apr. 1995, p. 3.

[42] *Jane's Defence Weekly*, 28 Feb. 1996, p. 12.

[43] Rybas (note 33), p. 6.

[44] Davydov, O., 'Osvaivaya novye mirovye rynki: Rossiya i Asiatsko–Tikhookeansky region' [Entering new world markets: Russia and the Asia–Pacific region], *Mezhdunarodnaya Zhizn*, no. 2 (1996), pp. 20–22; and Ivanov, V. I., 'Russia and the United States: still cold in Northeast Asia?', *Asia–Pacific Review*, autumn/winter 1995, pp. 107–10.

[45] Baliev, A., 'Obshchiye interesy velikikh sosedey' [Common interests of big neighbours], *Nezavisimoye Voyennoye Obozreniye*, no. 10 (1997).

Asia–Pacific markets. Direct trade links are being established with Australia, China, Hong Kong, Japan, North and South Korea, New Zealand, Singapore and the United States. In Primorskiy Kray (the Maritime Province) enterprises with some degree of foreign participation were in 1993 responsible for at least 10 per cent of exports. By mid-1994 in that province alone more than 800 enterprises were registered, with over $300 million of foreign funds invested. Exports from the Russian far east are rising. In 1993 the area's estimated share of national exports doubled and its exports exceeded $2 billion.[46] The region's total trade volume was $2.7 billion in 1992 and $3.2 billion in 1993. Its trade surplus in 1994 exceeded $1 billion. Asia–Pacific countries account for about 80 per cent of this trade, Japan being the leading market for traditional exports. As the importance of Russia's Pacific coast for the transit of goods increases, Russian ports are emerging as a base for re-export operations, particularly for trade with China and South Korea. Four major ports (Vostochniy, Vladivostok, Nakhodka and Vanino) together handle the same volume of foreign cargo as the three largest ports in European Russia (St Petersburg, Novorossiysk and Murmansk). In 1992–93, 46 per cent of all foreign cargo and 54 per cent of the high-value cargo in containers was channelled through Russia's Pacific coast ports.[47]

Several Russian and Chinese regions have developed very close economic relations and Chinese investment in the Russian far east has increased. In 1992–93 there were nearly 800 joint ventures and the number of exclusively Chinese enterprises has grown since then.[48] In fact, the southern part of the Russian far east and China's Dongbei province are interdependent, complementary economic areas.[49]

In 1994 the Russian central authorities launched a policy of 'new federalism' directed at providing the Russian regions with greater autonomy in economic matters and political administration. Russia, being unable to offer federal assistance to the regions, hopes that arms sales can help to foster economic reforms in its far eastern region, convert the local defence industry and attract foreign capital for reclamation of the area's natural resources. At a symposium spon-

---

[46] Ivanov (note 44), p. 107.

[47] Ivanov (note 44), p. 107.

[48] Menon (note 21), p. 104.

[49] Kerr, D., 'Opening and closing the Sino-Russian border: trade, regional development and political interest in North-East Asia', *Europe–Asia Studies,* vol. 48, no. 6 (1996), pp. 934–39.

sored by the National Defense University in Washington, a Russian diplomat, Yevgeniy Afanasyev, made it clear that Russia was eager to see 'the integration of [the] Russian far east and Siberia' into an economically dynamic East Asia, adding that such a development was an imperative that 'can accelerate our own economic reforms and development'.[50] Then Russian Foreign Minister Yevgeniy Primakov also told the leaders of members of the Association of South-East Asian Nations (ASEAN) in July 1996 that Russia was interested in establishing economic cooperation between the Russian far east and the South-East Asian countries.[51]

Public opinion and interest group politics

Military cooperation with the East Asian countries is important for Russia for domestic political reasons as well. Many people in the country feel humiliated and frustrated over Russia's loss of superpower status. To prove that Russia is still influential in international affairs, the Yeltsin Government portrays arms exports as an important and effective instrument of great-power policy.

Besides public opinion, some interest groups are influential in shaping Russia's East Asian policy. Two major lobbies are the military–industrial complex and the fuel and energy complex, which have both parallel and conflicting interests in the area. Their parallel interests are in penetrating the Asia–Pacific markets and developing friendly relations with particular countries and transnational organizations. Experience has shown the Russian elites that raw materials and military technology are about the only two Russian products for which substantial international demand exists.

Contention between the two interest groups stems from their different views on priorities in cooperation with East Asian countries. The military–industrial complex insists that priority should be given to military–technical programmes, arguing that the defence sector is the pinnacle of Russian science and technology and will serve as the 'locomotive' to pull the future recovery of the economy as a whole and that arms exports are the only way for Russia to regain its independence from the humiliation of Western aid. The fuel and energy complex claims that non-military cooperation with foreign countries is

[50] Cited in Ching (note 4), p. 32.
[51] *Diplomaticheskiy Vestnik,* no. 8 (1996), pp. 35–39.

more important for Russia's long-term interests because it creates a mechanism of interdependence in the area, thus strengthening regional stability, and that it is more profitable than the arms trade (civilian projects produce more offsets, and the capacity of the Asia–Pacific non-military market is increasing while arms acquisition is on the same level or possibly decreasing).

Neither the military–industrial nor the fuel and energy complex is a monolithic entity. Experts distinguish five main sectoral components of the Russian defence complex: manufacturers of military electronics, land-based weapon systems (such as artillery, tanks, armoured vehicles and small arms), aerospace, shipbuilding and the nuclear weapons industry. Of these the first, fourth and fifth sectors are doing badly. The second is hesitant whether to develop export-oriented production or conduct conversion. The aerospace sector is the most dynamic in adapting to market conditions. Its strategy of survival includes diversification of production, the formation of joint ventures and an aggressive export policy.[52] Its products, in particular fighter aircraft, are in demand on the East Asian markets.

Common interests do not preclude inter-sectoral competition even within the military–industrial complex. The shipbuilding and missile-producing sectors lobbied the government to strike a deal with Taiwan at the same time as the Su-27 deal was being discussed with China.[53] Sometimes there is even intra-sectoral competition. The companies which produce the MiG-29 and Su-27 fighter aircraft compete on the Chinese, Indian, Thai and Vietnamese markets.[54] The Irkutsk and Komsomolsk-na-Amure builders of the Su-27 clashed over the Chinese deal, as did the St Petersburg and Nizhniy Novgorod shipyards in the case of the contract with China for the Kilo Class submarine.[55]

According to some reports, the military–industrial complex was the first to form its own lobby both inside and outside the Russian Government. In the government of Yegor Gaidar (1991–92) several top officials represented the interests of the military–industrial complex: Georgiy Khizha, First Deputy Prime Minister; Viktor Glukhikh, Chairman of Goskomoboronprom; Vladimir Mikhailov, Chairman of

[52] Pappe (note 15), pp. 70–72.

[53] *Rossiyskaya Gazeta,* 4 Mar. 1992, p. 3; and *Izvestiya,* 14 Mar. 1992, p. 4.

[54] *Asian Defence Journal,* Dec. 1995, p. 131; and Beaver, P., 'China looks to Europe for carrier', *Jane's Intelligence Review and Jane's Sentinel Pointer,* Dec. 1996, p. 1.

[55] Scott, R., 'Kilo sale adds to Russia's exports', *Jane's Intelligence Review and Jane's Sentinel Pointer,* Oct. 1996, p. 1; and Markov, D., 'More details surface of Rubin's "Kilo" plans', *Jane's Intelligence Review,* May 1997, pp. 211, 215.

the Ministry of Atomic Industry; Igor Shurchkov, Chairman of Gosu-darstvenny Komitet po Promyshlennoy Politike (the State Committee on Industrial Policy); Sergey Glaziev, First Deputy Minister of Foreign Economic Relations; and Andrei Kokoshin, First Deputy Defence Minister.[56] All were proponents of resuming military ties with China and an active arms sale policy throughout the world.

The military–industrial complex has also formed lobbying organizations to push its interests in the political arena. The Association of Manufacturers and the Russian Union of Industrialists and Entrepreneurs were among them, but the main body representing the interests of the military–industrial complex has been the League of Assistance to Defence Enterprises, established in February 1992.[57]

The government used the arms trade as a bargaining instrument in its relations with the military–industrial complex. The latter was perceived by the 'democratic faction' of the Yeltsin team as a major source of internal threat to democratic reforms in the country and as a potential base for nationalist and pro-communist forces. Providing it with more access to the world arms markets could appease and divert it from confrontation with the government. Under pressure from the military–industrial complex, Russia resumed or enhanced military ties with former adversaries or 'rogue states' (China, Iran, Iraq and North Korea). Even security concerns stemming from the transfer of advanced technology were overruled in certain cases: some accounts suggest that the government agreed to the deal with China on co-production of the Su-27 under pressure from lobbyists.[58]

At the same time, the government had to take into account the growing power of the fuel and energy complex, initially underrepresented in the Yeltsin–Gaidar ruling elite. However, since Viktor Chernomyrdin, former Minister of Fuel and Energy and founder of the gas monopoly company Gazprom, took the posts of first deputy prime minister (May–June 1992) and then prime minister and head of the cabinet (December 1992–March 1998), the fuel and energy complex has become the most powerful lobby. Two close allies of Chernomyrdin—Yuriy Shafrannik and Vladimir Kvasov—assumed the positions of minister of fuel and energy and chief of the government's

---

[56] Pappe (note 15), p. 63.
[57] *Rossiyskaya Gazeta*, 28 Apr. 1997, p. 1.
[58] Menon (note 21), p. 112.

staff, respectively.[59] At the political level, the Russia Is Our Home coalition has become the leading representative of the fuel and energy complex.

Russia Is Our Home vigorously lobbied the government in favour of Sino-Russian non-military joint projects. For example, during his March 1997 visit to Beijing Alexander Shokhin, one of the leaders of Russia Is Our Home and First Deputy Chairman of the State Duma, put pressure on his Chinese counterparts to proceed with construction of a nuclear power station in Jiangsu (worth $2.5 billion) and to sign contracts on the construction of a thermoelectric power station in Beijing and a system of hydroelectric power stations on the Yangtse River (the Three Gorges project).[60] Rem Vyakhirev, Chairman of Gazprom and another key figure in Russia Is Our Home, told participants at the June 1997 Gas Congress in Copenhagen that his company expected growth in the Asian demand for gas to offer the biggest potential for exports. While big buyers such as Japan are a long way from some Gazprom fields in Siberia, much of Asia is not too far away, he said.[61] In particular, China and Russia are constructing a pipeline connecting the Irkutsk gas fields with the Chinese industrial centres (with the potential to extend it to other countries). The presidents of the two countries discussed this issue, among others, at their summit meetings in Beijing (April 1996) and Moscow (April 1997).[62]

Some analysts suggest that the position of the military–industrial complex within the Russian Government has weakened since 1991 while the influence of the fuel and energy complex was relatively stable under Chernomyrdin's premiership.[63] Many advocates of the military–industrial complex were forced to resign in 1993–94. It failed to form an influential faction in the State Duma after the elections of 1993 and 1995 and was unable to prevent the abolition of the key government bodies dealing with military production and arms exports—the state committees on military–technical policy (in August 1996) and defence industries (in March 1997).[64]

---

[59] Pappe (note 15), p. 65; and Temirkhanov, I., 'Gruppy davleniya v rossiyskoy politike' [Interest groups in Russian politics], *Ukraina Segodnya,* no. 7 (Sep.–Dec. 1994), pp. 40–41.

[60] *Dom i Otechestvo,* 6–14 Mar. 1997, p. 1.

[61] *International Herald Tribune,* 12 June 1997, p. 17.

[62] Fanlin, L., 'Strategicheskoye partnerstvo' [Strategic partnership], *Rossiyskaya Gazeta,* 22 Apr. 1997, p. 7.

[63] Pappe (note 15), pp. 64–65; Temirkhanov (note 59), pp. 51–52; and Rutland, P., 'Business lobbies in contemporary Russia', *International Spectator* (Rome), vol. 32, no. 1 (Jan.–Mar. 1997), p. 25.

[64] See chapter 3 in this volume.

It is not clear how these developments have affected arms export policies in East Asia. The Russian arms trade both in the region and worldwide was booming in the period 1993–97, regardless of the periodic government reshuffles and interest group competition.

Arms sales and the Russian post-communist security debate

The development of military cooperation with East Asia is not a question of temporary tactics or political contingency only. It is part of the fundamental debate on the strategic orientation of Russia's security policy in the age of post-communist transition.

There are several schools of foreign policy thought in Russia, differing both in their conceptual foundations and in their approaches to concrete international issues. These political and academic groups are, naturally, fluid coalitions: to reduce a complex debate to several categories may be to risk oversimplification. Such categories do, however, provide a helpful framework for analysing Russia's foreign policy discourse.

The Atlanticists

The Atlanticists (Westernizers) were in 1991–93 a relatively small group of highly placed government officials and academics close to the Ministry of Foreign Affairs. Their recognized leader was Andrey Kozyrev, former Foreign Minister. They consider that Western Europe and the United States should be the main orientation for Russian foreign policy and that Russia historically belongs to Western Christian civilization. The main task for Russian international strategy should be building a partnership with the West and joining Western economic, political and military institutions—the EU, NATO, the International Monetary Fund (IMF), the General Agreement on Tariffs and Trade (GATT, now replaced by the World Trade Organization) and the Group of Seven industrialized countries (G7).[65] In an article in *NATO Review* Kozyrev stressed that Russia's main guideline was to 'join the club of recognized democratic states with market economies, on a basis of equality'.[66] He regarded such a partnership as the principal source of international support for Russian reforms.

[65] Russia joined the G7 at its Birmingham meeting in May 1998; with the participation of Russia, it is referred to as the G8.

[66] *NATO Review,* Feb. 1993, p. 3.

During that period Russia refrained from opposing NATO enlargement. The Atlanticists maintained that, combined with the Conference on Security and Co-operation in Europe (CSCE), as it then was called,[67] NATO could become the starting-point for the formation of a new type of Euro-Atlantic community which could guarantee international stability from Vancouver to Vladivostok.

The Atlanticists occupied key positions in government. In addition to Kozyrev there were Prime Minister Gaidar, State Secretary Gennadiy Burbulis, Minister of Communications Mikhail Poltoranin, and deputy foreign ministers Vitaly Churkin, Georgiy Kunadze and Fyodor Shilov-Kovedyayev.[68] From the very beginning of his career as Russian leader, Yeltsin's foreign policy was pro-US and pro-Western. Russia reduced its arms exports in exchange for Western promises of financial and technical assistance. However, a new geopolitical situation after the breakdown of the USSR and other international and domestic developments caused a crisis in the Atlanticist school of thought and a shift to traditional strategic concepts.

In the event the USA and the EU were not responsive to Russia's demands for large-scale economic assistance and participation in the Western economic and politico-military institutions. Moreover, the West often ignored Russia's position on important security questions such as the tempo and conditions of the pull-out of Russian troops from the former Warsaw Treaty Organization (WTO) countries and the Baltic states, the rights of national minorities in the 'near abroad', NATO enlargement, the conflict in Yugoslavia, the sale of cryogenic missile engines to India, the nuclear deal with Iran, or the sale of Su-27 aircraft to China. Thus, the West did not accept Russia as a part of Europe or of Western civilization in general. On a number of occasions Yeltsin and Kozyrev complained of a 'non-constructive' policy on the part of the USA.

In addition, bloody national conflicts along the southern borders of Russia changed Russia's security philosophy. It was in relation to the 'near abroad' that the Russian leadership started to define its strategic interests, to speak of spheres of influence and to express concern about a possible power vacuum to be filled by hostile powers. In fact, Russia elaborated a sort of Russian Monroe Doctrine when Yeltsin in February 1993 laid claim to responsibility for maintaining peace and

[67] The CSCE became the Organization for Security and Co-operation in Europe on 1 Jan. 1995.

[68] *Nezavisimaya Gazeta,* 30 July 1992, pp. 1, 3, and 27 Mar. 1993, p. 1.

stability in the whole post-Soviet space and Kozyrev applied to the international community (the UN and the Organization for Security and Co-operation in Europe, OSCE) to grant Russia an international mandate for peacekeeping in the geographical area of the former Soviet Union.[69]

Facing potential NATO enlargement, the Kremlin launched a political campaign aimed both at fostering military cooperation within the Commonwealth of Independent States (CIS) and at finding new (or relatively new) strategic allies in the East, such as China and India.

These developments resulted in a reduction of the Atlanticists' influence on Russian foreign policy and a shift of their leaders (including Kozyrev) closer to nationalistic positions.

Moreover, the Atlanticists split into two groups. While Kozyrev's followers became more assertive vis-à-vis the West and neo-imperialist as to the 'near abroad', a number of liberal politicians, academics and journalists were in favour of 'civilized dialogue' both with the West and with the newly independent countries of the former Soviet Union. They were also nervous about too rapid a rapprochement with China and other Asian countries.[70]

In 1994–95 the Atlanticists were unable to act as a united political force. At the political level, however, they were able to sell some ideas to some liberal and reformist organizations and election coalitions (Chernomyrdin's Russia is Our Home; Yabloko, led by Grigoriy Yavlinskiy and Vladimir Lukin; Russia's Democratic Choice, led by Yegor Gaidar; and the Party of Russian Unity and Accord, headed by First Deputy Prime Minister Sergey Shakhrai).

The Eurasianists

The Eurasianist concept (*evraziistvo* in Russian) became popular among Russian intellectuals in the 1990s and was the first serious alternative to the pro-Western theories which were dominant in Russian security thinking in the late 1980s and early 1990s. The concept drew heavily on a philosophical school of 1920s Russian émigrés who had tried to find a compromise with the Stalinist version of

<hr>

[69] Litera, B., 'The Kozyrev Doctrine: a Russian variation on the Monroe Doctrine', *Perspectives*, winter 1994/95, pp. 45–52.

[70] Arbatov, A., 'Imperiya ili velikaya derzhava?' [Empire or great power?], *Novoye Vremya*, no. 49 (Dec. 1992), pp. 16–18; *Novoye Vremya*, no. 50 (Dec. 1992), pp. 20–23; Goncharov, S., 'Osobye interesy Rossii: chto eto takoye?' [Russia's special interests: what are they?], *Izvestiya*, 25 Feb. 1992, p. 3; and Trush (note 3).

socialism. It stresses the uniqueness of Russia, one of its key postulates being that in civilizational terms Russia has never been a part of Europe.[71] Hence, it should choose a 'third way' between the West and the East. Globally, Russia was to be a bridge between these civilizations.

Contemporary proponents of this theory divide into two opposing groups, the reformist or democratic camp and the Slavophiles.

The democrats have tried to adapt Eurasianism to their views for a number of reasons. First, they realized their own weakness in terms of neglecting the national question and Russian national values. The nationalists and the communists were obviously stronger in this field, and thus in part managed to capture people's sympathy by appealing to their humiliation over their loss of national dignity. According to a well-known Russian writer, Leonid Vasilev, the democrats have had to try to reclaim the national, cultural and historical legacy which the patriots have tried to claim for themselves.[72] Obviously, the adoption of Eurasianism by the democrats was part of a strategy aimed at conquering both Russian public opinion and the political elite.

Second, Eurasianism was a reaction of democrats disappointed by the West's reluctance to admit Russia to its institutions and by the scale of Western assistance to Russia. They realized that it was unwise to rely too heavily on the West. By adhering to Eurasianism they tried to demonstrate to the West that it could well lose a potential ally.

Third, Eurasianism reflected the geopolitical position of Russia and the need to maintain stable relations to its east and south. At a meeting at the Russian Foreign Ministry in February 1992, Sergey Stankevich, then adviser to the president, said: 'There is no getting away from certain facts. One of them is that we are now separated from Europe by a whole chain of independent states and find ourselves much further from it, which inevitably involves a definite and, indeed, a quite substantial redistribution of our resources, our potentialities, our links and our interests in favour of Asia and the Eastern sector'.[73]

The Eurasianists believed that the government had overemphasized the West and that Russia's most compelling needs were in the south

---

[71] Fedotov, G. P., *Sudba i Grekhi Rossii* [The destiny and sins of Russia] (Sofiya: St Petersburg, 1991), vols 1–2; Karsavin, L., 'Osnovy politiki' [Fundamentals of politics], *Evraziyskiy Vremennik* (Paris), issue 5 (1927); and Trubetskoi, N. S., 'Russkaya problema' [The Russian problem], *Evraziyskaya Khronika* (Prague), issue 1 (1925).

[72] Jonson, L., 'In search of a national interest: the foreign policy debate in Russia', *Nationalities Papers,* vol. 22, no. 1 (spring 1994).

[73] *International Affairs* (Moscow), vol. 39, no. 1 (Jan. 1993), p. 48.

and east, on the 'arc of crisis' developing on its southern borders and in relations with its own sizeable Muslim population. Russia, they argued, has to develop an active diplomacy to meet the challenges posed by Iran, Saudi Arabia, Turkey and other Islamic countries, and coping with these threats and challenges is more important than maintaining an active dialogue with the West on European and transatlantic issues.

The Eurasianist approach gave priority to the consolidation of economic, political and security ties between the countries of the former Soviet Union, preferably within the context of the CIS. In defining the Eurasianist concept of security regarding the 'near abroad', Vladimir Lukin, then Russian Ambassador to the United States, called it a Russian variation on the 'good neighbour' policy.[74]

East Asia was also crucial for the Eurasianists' geopolitical vision. A number of prosperous countries such as Japan, South Korea and some of the ASEAN countries could be promising trade partners and a source of investment for Russia's troubled economy.[75] Moreover, military cooperation with China and India could be important pillars for the new Eurasian security complex.[76] 'Russia must put its political and economic relations with China on an equal footing to its relations with Europe and the United States. Russia's goal here should be to establish an "irreversible interdependence" in which neither country could return to a policy of direct confrontation with the other.'[77]

At the same time, this faction of the Eurasianists does not deny the importance of maintaining good relations with the West. They do not object to Russia entering either the international economy or the 'defence structure of the advanced part of the world community'.[78]

The main point in the Eurasianists' dispute with the Atlanticists has been the need to adjust the balance between the Western and Eastern directions of Russia's international strategy. As one advocate of Eurasianism explained, 'Partnership with the West will undoubtedly

[74] Lukin, V. P., 'Russia and its interests', ed. S. Sestanovich, *Rethinking Russia's National Interests* (Center for Strategic and International Studies: Washington, DC, 1994), p. 109.

[75] Sarkisov, K., 'Russia and Japan', eds R. D. Blackwill and S. A. Karaganov, Center for Science and International Affairs, Harvard University, *Damage Limitation or Crisis? Russia and the Outside World*, CSIA Studies in International Security no. 5 (Brassey's: Washington, DC/London, 1994), p. 262.

[76] Miasnikov, V. S., 'Russia and China', eds Blackwill and Karaganov (note 75), pp. 228–38.

[77] Lukin (note 74), p. 110.

[78] Bogaturov, A. D., Kozhokin, M. M. and Pleshakov, K. V., 'Vneshnyaya politika Rossii' [Russia's foreign policy], *USA: Economics, Politics, Ideology*, no. 10 (1992), p. 31.

strengthen Russia in its relations with the East and the South, while partnership with the East and the South will give Russia independence in its contacts with the West'.[79]

Initially, the Eurasianists were much less influential than the Atlanticists in the Yeltsin Government and Russian political elites. However, as discontent with Kozyrev's pro-Western line increased, they became stronger among policy makers and foreign policy experts. Along with Stankevich and Lukin, the leading figures most closely associated with this view have been Nikolay Travkin, leader of the Democratic Party of Russia; Anatoliy Sobchak, former mayor of St Petersburg; and Yevgeniy Ambartsumov, head of the Committee on International Affairs of the Supreme Soviet of the Russian Federation.[80]

Starting to coalesce in 1992, the Eurasianist democrats were by 1993 able to influence the security debates in Russia. The theoretical framework of Russia's 1993 foreign policy doctrine (especially the setting of regional priorities) was clearly influenced by Eurasianist ideas.[81] The nationalists and the Eurasianists were together successful in forcing Kozyrev to pay more attention to the CIS and Asia–Pacific. President Yeltsin echoed their themes during his 1992 visit to India, emphasizing Russia's Eurasian identity when he pointed out that the greater part of Russia's territory lies in Asia and that most Russian citizens live in the Asian part of Russia.[82]

In contrast, the Slavophiles played down Russia's unique geopolitical position but stressed its distinctiveness from both West and East. Elgiz Pozdnyakov, a Russian authority on international relations theory, noted: 'The geopolitical location of Russia is not just unique (so is that of any state), it is truly fateful for both herself and the world . . . An important aspect of this situation was that Russia, being situated between two civilisations, was a natural keeper of both a civilised equilibrium and a world balance of power'.[83]

---

[79] Cited in Malcolm, N., 'New thinking and after: debate in Moscow about Europe', ed. N. Malcolm, Royal Institute of International Affairs (RIIA), *Russia and Europe: An End to Confrontation?* (Pinter: London and New York, 1994), p. 167.

[80] Dawisha, K. and Parrott, P., *Russia and the States of Eurasia: The Politics of Upheaval* (Cambridge University Press: Cambridge, 1994), pp. 200–201.

[81] Russian Ministry of Foreign Affairs, 'Kontseptsiya vneshney politiki Rossiyskoy Federatsii' [Foreign policy concept of the Russian Federation], *Diplomaticheskiy Vestnik*, Special Issue (Jan. 1993), pp. 3–23.

[82] Singh (note 4), p. 71

[83] Pozdnyakov, E., 'Russia is a great power', *International Affairs* (Moscow), vol. 39, no. 1 (Jan. 1993), p. 6.

According to the Slavophiles, this determined in no small measure the evolution of the Russian state as a great power and the establishment of a strong central authority. Unlike the democrats, the Slavophiles have not been frightened of calling Russia an empire and supporting its revival. 'Russia has always been held together by a strong system of state power . . . I have no doubt that guaranteeing Russia's existence is a top priority today. This can only be done by a strong authority equal to saving the people from arbitrary practices, anarchy, hunger and civil war. This must extend to the whole nation.'[84]

In contrast to the democrats, the Slavophiles opposed Western assistance. They considered it irrelevant and burdensome and proposed reliance upon Russia's own resources. They opposed Russia's joining Western economic, political and military institutions on the grounds that this would restrict the country's sovereignty and favoured making the protection of Russian minorities in the former Soviet republics a top foreign policy priority. Also in contrast to the democrats, they did not rule out the use of force to defend these minorities.

Representatives of this faction have been scattered among many different political parties and groups. The Slavophiles have tended to be grouped around some newspapers and journals—*Den*, *Nash Sovremennik* and *Molodaya Gvardiya*. Politically, they have been organized in associations and election coalitions such as the Russian National Assembly (Sobor) and the Congress of Russian Communities.

By the end of 1993 both versions of Eurasianism—democratic and Slavophile—found themselves, like Atlanticism, in a critical situation because of a number of intellectual and political factors.

The derzhavniki

As a result of the success of the radical populist Vladimir Zhirinovsky in the December 1993 elections, the domestic basis for a pro-Western policy shrank. The conservative faction of the Atlanticists (including Kozyrev) and the democratic wing of the Eurasianists merged into the group of *derzhavniki* or *gosudarstvenniki*—proponents of a strong and powerful state which can maintain order and serve as a guarantee against anarchy and instability, a rather traditional Russian view of the state's role.

---

[84] Pozdnyakov, E., 'Russia today and tomorrow', *International Affairs* (Moscow), vol. 39, no. 2 (Feb. 1993), p. 30.

The *derzhavniki* opposed the idea that a choice had to be made between a pro-Western and a pro-Asian line in foreign policy. They believed that Russia is both a European and an Asian country and that the best way to define its identity was to become Russian and to respect the nation's own history and values.[85]

Along with the democratic Eurasianists they considered the CIS and the 'near abroad' as the top priority for Russia's security policy. The so-called Kozyrev Doctrine, proclaimed by the Russian Foreign Minister in a speech to Russian diplomatic representatives in the CIS and the Baltic states in January 1994, became a symbol of the *derzhavniki* foreign policy concept. He declared that the vital strategic issue for Russian diplomacy was the defence of Russian minority rights in the 'near abroad'. He affirmed the need for a Russian military presence in this area and advocated the idea of dual nationality.[86]

This group favoured better relations with the West, but not at the cost of diminishing Russia's role as an independent great power with its own spheres of influence. Policy towards the West became more assertive. Some Western experts, however, pointed out that:

The neo-imperialist bark has been worse than its bite; aggressiveness has been more a matter of words than deeds. This discrepancy is in all likelihood due to the fact that several of the *derzhavniki*, Kozyrev among them, are essentially sheep in wolves' clothing. They retain a fundamentally Western outlook but feel obliged to make verbal concessions and tactical adjustments to changes in popular mood and pressures exerted from within the political establishment.[87]

The *derzhavniki* remain fairly sceptical about the West's willingness and ability to help Russia realize its reforms. They argue against excessive reliance on Western economic assistance and political guidance and advocate an active arms export policy regardless of Western opposition. They do not oppose cooperation by the military–industrial complex with rival countries. As competition in the international arms and high-technology markets intensifies throughout the world, mergers are becoming more common and international strategic alliances are being formed to make products more competitive. 'Russia today

---

[85] Vladislavlev, A. and Karaganov, S., 'The idea of Russia', *International Affairs* (Moscow), vol. 38, no. 12 (Dec. 1992), p. 31.

[86] *Nezavisimaya Gazeta,* 19 Jan. 1994, p. 1; and Litera (note 69), pp. 45–52.

[87] Adomeit, H., 'Russia as a great power in world affairs: images and reality', *International Affairs* (London), vol. 71, no. 1 (1995), p. 59.

cannot keep its doors closed to new technology because in future it will have to compete on the armaments market against the conglomerates of Western countries, as well as those of Asian countries.'[88]

The *derzhavniki* favour developing friendly relations with countries such as China, India, Japan and South Korea but warn against illusions as to the possible extent of rapprochement with them, pointing out their preoccupation with their own affairs and a number of serious problems in bilateral relations, for example, the border disputes with China, Chinese illegal migration to the Russian far east and the Kuril Islands issue in relations with Japan.[89] Some *derzhavniki* have suggested that in the long run a strategic association between Russia and the West, as well as Japan and South Korea, is not only advisable but possible. In the short term, such an association could only function in a relatively narrow military–political and geo-strategic sphere.[90]

The pro-Eastern bias of Russian foreign policy increased with the arrival of Primakov as Foreign Minister in early 1996, an expert in oriental studies and loyal to the principles of the *derzhavniki* foreign policy doctrine. Unlike Kozyrev, he launched a vigorous policy of establishing economic ties between the Russian far east and the rest of East Asia, as well as demonstrating to the West Russia's capability as a counterweight to the enlargement of NATO and the EU.

The moderate liberals

A number of political groups which were disappointed with the pro-Western bias of Atlanticism, the south-eastern orientation of Eurasianism, and the neo-imperialist and paternalist course of the *derzhavniki* finally formed a rather elusive moderate faction. They are in favour of cooperation with both the West and the East but suggest putting Russia's national interest and democratic values at the heart of its security policy.

The liberals have noted Russia's current weakness and declining role in East Asia. Sergey Rogov, Director of the Institute of USA and Canada Studies of the Russian Academy of Sciences, has admitted that some of the former Soviet republics could be drawn into the spheres of interest of such regional centres of power as China or

<hr>

[88] First Deputy Defence Minister Andrey Kokoshin, cited in Perera, J., 'Russian arms sales in 1996 over US $3 billion', *Jane's Intelligence Review and Jane's Sentinal Pointer*, Apr. 1997, p. 2.

[89] Vladislavlev and Karaganov (note 85), p. 34.

[90] Blackwill and Karaganov (note 75), p. 23.

Japan.[91] Alexei Arbatov, Deputy Chairman of the Duma Committee on Defence, has even suggested that China may represent the greatest external security threat to Russia in the long run.[92] He and other moderate liberals do not approve of too quick a military rapprochement with China and warn of the possibility of Russia becoming one-sidedly dependent on China.[93]

For that reason, Arbatov observes, the interests of Russia in the region may be best served by the maintenance of the political role and limited military presence of the United States.[94] If the United States were to withdraw, the Japanese reaction could be none other than remilitarization in view of the rapid growth of economic and military power in China. A clash between these two giants could draw Russia into the conflict as well. In addition to keeping a US military presence, Russia's national interests would be best served by a new multilateral security system in the region.

Arbatov believes that Russia should eventually transfer the disputed Kuril Islands to Japan as part of a fundamental revision of political and security relations between the two countries. A new security regime based on arms reductions and confidence-building measures could be created in the Western Pacific. Economic cooperation between Russia and Japan could follow, provided that Russia creates attractive conditions for foreign investments in Siberia and East Asia. Russia should also promote the reunification of Korea in order to eliminate this source of serious tension in the region.[95]

As for military cooperation with China, the liberals (in particular some experts close to the Yabloko Party, led by Yavlinskiy and Lukin) have three main concerns. First, they fear that in the distant future a Chinese military build-up could be directed not only against Japan, Taiwan and the United States but also against Russia.[96] Second, they point out that Sino-Russian military rapprochement makes the West nervous and could damage Russia's relations with the latter.[97]

---

[91] Rogov, S., 'A national security policy for Russia', eds J. E. Goodby and B. Morel, SIPRI, *The Limited Partnership: Building a Russian–US Security Community* (Oxford University Press: Oxford, 1993), p. 76.

[92] Arbatov, A., 'Russian national interests', eds Blackwill and Karaganov (note 75), p. 72.

[93] Arbatov (note 92); and Trush (note 3).

[94] Arbatov (note 92), p. 72.

[95] Arbatov (note 92), p. 73.

[96] Trenin (note 3), p. 4.

[97] Trush (note 3). See also Larin, V., 'Rossiya i Kitay na poroge tretyego tysyacheletiya: kto zhe budet otstaivat nashy natsionalnye interesy?' [Russia and China on the threshold of

They suggest a more cautious and consistent arms sales policy in the region. Third, they stress that technology transfer will enable China to export Chinese versions of Russian weapon systems, thus undercutting Russia in the global arms market.[98]

Some analysts are against arms exports to the region for ideological and moral reasons. They consider the arms trade an amoral and dirty business which provokes regional arms races and local conflicts. They believe that intensive arms exports support the military–industrial complex and therefore its influence on Russian domestic politics.[99]

The neo-communists

There are several pro-communist groups in contemporary Russia. They vary from neo-Stalinist to socialist-like organizations. The Communist Party of the Russian Federation (CPRF), led by Gennadiy Zyuganov, is the strongest among them. However, despite its influential role in domestic politics, the CPRF lacks a well-articulated and positive foreign policy platform. It prefers to criticize the former Soviet and current Russian leadership rather than produce a new conceptual departure itself.

The communists believe that Russia is part of neither the West nor the East. It should define its own, independent way. At the same time they are not really drawn to Eurasianism, regarding both Russian and world history as a result of objective processes rather than messianistic ideas. However, they acknowledge the need for a national ideal or doctrine that could consolidate Russian society. They emphasize the country's national interests, which do not depend on a regime or dominant ideology; they believe that Russia's main national interests derive from its history and consist in preserving its territorial and spiritual integrity. The idea of a powerful state based on multi-ethnicity is equivalent to the Russian national idea. Thus, the breakdown of the Soviet Union and the weakening of the Russian state have undermined Russia's security and hurt its geo-strategic position.

As for other regions, the communists have proposed restoring Russia's links with its 'traditional friends and allies' such as Cuba,

---

the third millennium: who will protect our national interests?], *Problemy Dalnego Vostoka*, no. 1 (1997), pp. 15–26.

[98] Menon (note 21), p. 112.

[99] See, e.g., Avduevsky (note 37), pp. 7–10.

Iraq, North Korea and Libya.[100] This could prevent the USA from winning unchallenged world leadership and provide Russia with profitable orders for its troubled arms industry. They accepted détente in Sino-Russian relations as well as an active arms export policy in the region because it would add to Russia's international authority and support the defence industry. Many leaders of the CPRF are attracted to the Chinese model of socialism and believe that Gorbachev should have used China's experience to reform the Soviet Union.[101] At the same time, the CPRF is concerned about the future security orientation of China and the ratio of forces in Asia–Pacific, which is turning out to be rather unfavourable for Russia.[102]

The right radicals

There are several extremist organizations in Russia, united primarily by their rejection of Yeltsin's domestic reforms and by criticism of his pro-Western foreign policy. At the same time there are also major disagreements about both the meaning of Russian history and the appropriate model for the future. Hence they have been unable to go beyond negativism and develop a coherent, forward-looking agenda of their own.

The Liberal Democratic Party of Russia (LDPR), led by Vladimir Zhirinovsky, is the most important of the right radical organizations. The LDPR was the largest in the Duma during 1993–95 and still has influential positions in the parliament elected in December 1995. It is difficult to reconstruct Zhirinovsky's foreign policy concept because of its lack of elementary logic, the extravagant form of expression of his ideas and the fact that his statements often contradict one another. Zhirinovsky opposes Russia receiving foreign aid and told US reporters: 'We need no help from the United States or the West! . . . We are a very rich country'.[103] He also opposes Russia's giving aid to other countries, with the exception of Iraq and Serbia. He opposes defence industry conversion in Russia and strongly advocates sales of Russian arms abroad. On a number of occasions he has expressed anti-US and anti-Western sentiments and appealed to the nation to

---

[100] 'Election 1995: parties' foreign policy views', *International Affairs* (Moscow), vol. 41, nos 11–12 (1995), p. 9.

[101] Pushkov, A., 'Chinese mirage', *Moscow News,* no. 22 (1995), p. 4.

[102] Zyuganov, G., *Za Gorizontom* [Over the horizon] (Veshniye Vody: Orel, 1995), p. 87.

[103] *Washington Times,* 14 Jan. 1994, p. A12.

regain its superpower status. He also suggests the immediate use of military force to protect the Russian minorities in the former Soviet republics and of economic sanctions against those countries which are not in line with Russia's course.

East Asia is not very important for the leader of the LDPR. His attention is focused mainly on the Balkans and the Middle East. Zhirinovsky proclaimed as a geopolitical concept the necessity for Russia to gain access to the Mediterranean Sea and the Indian Ocean by military conquest.[104] In an interview he projected a trilateral German–Russian–Indian axis, linking an expanded Germany, a new Russia that would include most of the former Soviet Union and some additional territory, and India—some 2 billion people. He imagined that the world would take on whatever form this axis imposed upon it. India and Russia together could neutralize China, and Germany and Russia could either neutralize or control Europe.[105] Zhirinovsky considers China the main threat to Russia in East Asia. He is against arming China with Russian weapons and is especially concerned about the transfer of technology and production rights. The Liberal Democrats insist on the 'containment' of China instead of its 'appeasement',[106] fear Chinese 'ethnic aggression' against the Russian far east, and favour using tough economic, administrative and military methods to stop China.[107]

The LDPR favours a more assertive position regarding the territorial claims of neighbouring countries (including China and Japan). For example, Zhirinovsky told Japanese journalists: 'You'd better not raise the Kurile Islands issue, otherwise we'll bring up the issue of compensation for the 40 years of illegal use of Sakhalin by Japan . . . We'll drive everyone out of the Sea of Okhotsk—the Japanese, the Koreans, the [Filipinos] . . . The Sea of Okhotsk will be a closed Russian sea. We'll establish a 200-mile zone, and you'll be fishing in Australia'.[108]

[104] Zhirinovsky, V., *Posledniy Brosok na Yug* [Last dash to the south] (LDPR: Moscow, 1993).

[105] Morrison, J. W., *Vladimir Zhirinovskiy: An Assessment of a Russian Ultra-Nationalist* (National Defense University: Washington, DC, 1994), pp. 110–11.

[106] Zhirinovsky (note 104); and 'Election 1995: parties' foreign policy views' (note 100), pp. 15–16.

[107] 'Election 1995: parties' foreign policy views' (note 100), p. 13.

[108] Interfax, 'Threatens to close Sea of Okhotsk', 6 Jan. 1997 (in English), in FBIS-SOV-94-005, 7 Jan. 1994, p. 10.

Despite the influence of the Liberal Democrats in domestic affairs, their impact on foreign policy issues has been moderate. The 'Zhirinovsky phenomenon' shifted Russian security debates slightly to the right but has had no direct effect on official foreign policy and military doctrines or on theoretical discourse.

In summary, despite the covert or overt opposition of the foreign policy schools of thought, the vast majority of Russian political groups and experts are strongly in favour of military cooperation with East Asia.

III. The international environment

Although they play an important role, economic and other domestic incentives are not the only reasons for Russian military–technical cooperation with the countries of the region. A number of geopolitical, strategic, security and humanitarian issues make East Asia crucial for Russia's national interest.

Global changes

According to official foreign policy doctrine, East Asia is important for Russia. In the Russian Foreign Ministry document of 1993 it ranked sixth on a list of 15 priorities, after the CIS, arms control and international security, economic reform, the United States and Europe.[109] In February 1996 the new foreign minister, Primakov, elevated East Asia to third position in his system of priorities (after the CIS and Eastern Europe). The Russian leadership has repeatedly emphasized that Russia has always been a Euro-Asian country, with regard not only to its territory but also to its interests, policies and even psychology.[110] The arms trade is perceived by policy makers as one of the most effective foreign policy tools to achieve both tactical and strategic goals.

Russian strategists believe that East Asia will play a special part in the processes determining the world's destiny. The powerful growth and enormous potential of the region could be a force for the creation of the world economy and in overcoming the strikingly uneven char-

[109] Russian Ministry of Foreign Affairs (note 81), pp. 3–23.

[110] Bogaturov, Kozhokin and Pleshakov (note 78), p. 31; *International Affairs* (Moscow), vol. 39, no. 1 (Jan. 1993), p. 48; and Singh (note 4), p. 71.

acter of economic development and income in the modern world.[111] The economic success of the young industrial states to a certain extent answers one of the fundamental questions of our times. It shows that former colonies and dependent territories are quite capable of economic creativity in modern conditions. In effect these states are paving the way for other developing countries.[112] The same applies to democratic institutions and forms of social life, the ultimate assertion of which in East Asia—along with full implementation of human rights—would mean another major defeat of totalitarianism after the transformation in Eastern Europe and the former USSR.

For these reasons Russia is trying to keep a high profile and to control developments in the area.

Security issues

East Asia has and will continue to have a weighty say in the sphere of military security. With its hundreds of millions of people and dozens of nationalities, outstanding contradictions and territorial disputes, the region is truly crucial for both Russian and world security.

Kozyrev made it clear, for instance at the ASEAN Annual Ministerial Meeting and the ensuing Post Ministerial Conference in July 1993, that Russia views its arms sales as a means of entering into the dialogue on Asian security issues and as a move towards restructuring the Asian security order, for example, by establishing an arms trade code, as he had been urging since early 1993.[113] Pointing out that two-thirds of Russian territory lies within Asia, another Russian diplomat said: 'we cannot agree with any attempts by any country to diminish Russia's role in the region or to limit its influence on the topical issues in the area'.[114] In recent years a Russian temptation to play the 'Chinese card' against Japan and the USA could be explained in part by its isolation from the principal economic and security institutions gradually being developed in the region.

Russia shares a number of security interests with some East Asian countries. For instance, like Russia, China tries to remain vigilant against the two threats to its security in the post-cold war era: Islamic

[111] Trenin (note 3), p. 1.
[112] Brutens, K., *Russia and the Asian–Pacific Region* (RAND/UCLA Center for Soviet Studies: Santa Monica, Calif., 1992), p. 4.
[113] Blank (note 5), pp. 43–44.
[114] Ching (note 4), p. 32.

fundamentalism and resurgent regional powers. While Russia is afraid of an Islamic threat to its southern borders, officials in Beijing suspect that Iran or the Central Asian nations might try to export Islamic fundamentalism to western China. Xinjiang province is considered to be particularly susceptible to such influences.[115] Russian arms could help China keep separatist movements under control. Some reports suggest that China's April 1996 strategic accord on confidence building in the military field in border areas with Kazakhstan, Kyrgyzstan, Russia and Tajikistan, aimed at preventing military clashes along its frontiers, may also restrict the flow of arms from Afghanistan to Muslim separatist rebels in Xinjiang.[116] Separatist activities combined with Tibetan unrest are at present forcing China to maintain 16 divisions in a state of alert in the neighbouring Lanzhou region. Arms smugglers start from Talogan, the mujahideen/Tajik headquarters in Afghanistan, then slip past Russian guards on the Afghan/Tajik frontier. They traverse the high Pamir Mountains, cross the Chinese frontier and arrive at Kashgar in Xinjiang. China hopes that the treaty will bring increased Russian and Tajik cooperation with its own frontier guards in policing the border against unlawful elements.

Both Russia and China are also concerned about military threats stemming from some of their neighbours, particularly Japan. In a sense, for the past 100 years Japan has assumed what China saw as its own proper role in the world, and today the Chinese security elites see Japan's economic and technological capability as being easily transformed into a modern indigenous military production capacity that would provide the economic and military strength required for regional pre-eminence. Following the US military draw-down in East Asia and the Western Pacific, China believes that an 'unbridled Japan . . . [might] seek to transform its enormous economic power into military strength'.[117]

If the US military draw-down continues, Japan will have the largest number of major surface combatants in Asia with the most modern capabilities. It will also have the most effective anti-submarine warfare capability and the most modern air force. Chinese security specialists often express genuine concern about the Sino-Japanese

---

[115] Rumer, B., 'The gathering storm in Central Asia', *Orbis*, winter 1993, p. 90.

[116] *Jane's International Defense Review*, Aug. 1996, p. 13; and *SIPRI Yearbook 1997: Armaments, Disarmament and International Security* (Oxford University Press: Oxford, 1997), p. 549.

[117] Brick, A., 'The Asian giants: neighborly ambivalence', *Global Affairs*, fall 1991, p. 84.

strategic balance in the 21st century. For leaders throughout the Asia–Pacific region, there is no doubt that the most significant aspect of the Japanese–US security alliance is that it serves to limit any Japanese sense of insecurity or impulse to develop an independent security role, with all the undesirable regional consequences.[118]

The 1997 Guidelines for US–Japan Defense Cooperation[119] have raised security concerns in many East Asian capitals, despite Japanese and US assurances that they are not aimed at any particular country. According to some accounts, the new guidelines appear to allow Japan to provide assistance if the USA dispatches troops in an emergency to the Korean peninsula, the Taiwan Straits, the disputed Spratly Islands or anywhere else in areas surrounding Japan.[120] The guidelines do not include a combat role for Japan, but could lead to Japan deploying minesweepers outside combat areas or repairing US aircraft and ships.

China has told Japan to 'learn the lessons of history' and avoid destabilizing the Asia–Pacific region. The South Korean Foreign Ministry said it would not tolerate Japanese troops on its soil and demanded to know the details of the new pact.[121] Japan sent diplomats to Beijing and Seoul to try to ease fears about the new agreement.

Russia is also interested in peaceful resolution of the Spratly Islands dispute because, on the one hand, it involves a number of countries which could be promising trade partners and, on the other hand, it destabilizes the region. In addition, Russia would welcome any joint efforts to fight piracy in the area.

Bilateral relations

Russia believes that its partners' interest in military cooperation will favour the further development of stable bilateral relationships and ease the resolution of any other problems that arise. For example, Russian arms transfers to South Korea have helped to resolve the problem of Russia's debt.

[118] Godwin, P. and Schulz, J., 'China and arms control: transition in East Asia', *Arms Control Today*, Nov. 1994, p. 8.

[119] US–Japan Subcommittee for Defense Cooperation, *Guidelines for US–Japan Defense Cooperation'*, New York, 23 Sep. 1997, available from the US Defense Department DefenseLINK Internet site at URL <http://www.defenselink.mil>.

[120] Richardson, M., 'A "critical moment" for security', *International Herald Tribune*, 10 June 1997, p. 7.

[121] *International Herald Tribune*, 11 June 1997, pp. 5, 10.

Sino-Russian military cooperation has created a favourable atmosphere for the resolution of territorial disputes between the two countries. Despite some security concerns among elements of the Russian military and some politicians, the Yeltsin Government and a majority of defence experts are confident that China will not use its growing military potential against Russia as it has in the recent past.[122] During his visit to China in May 1995, former Russian Defence Minister Pavel Grachev responded to some domestic critics that China will never again pose a military threat to Russia.[123] The Russian leadership has also pointed out that arms and technology transfers promote other forms of economic cooperation between the two countries. In 1993, 1994, 1995 and 1996 Sino-Russian bilateral trade amounted to $7.68 billion, $5.1 billion, $5.14 billion and $6.85 billion, respectively[124]—the total amount of which is more than the value of the entire Sino-Soviet trade during the 1950s and 1960s. China became Russia's third-largest trading partner after Germany and the United States,[125] and the Russian and Chinese presidents have said that they aim to increase bilateral trade to $20 billion per year by the turn of the century.[126] A number of Russian regions and particular enterprises have established direct connections with their Chinese counterparts. In turn, this commercial and industrial infrastructure serves as an additional spur to the development of Sino-Russian cooperation in other areas.

In other words, Russia has a number of very serious incentives—both domestic and international—to foster military cooperation with the East Asian countries.

[122] Afanasiev, E., 'Russia–China relations: from normalization to partnership', *Far Eastern Affairs* (Moscow), no. 1 (1994), pp. 3–8.

[123] In contrast with Grachev, Kotelkin of Rosvooruzheniye commented that 'developing military and technical co-operation with China, Russia will not leave China's geopolitical aspirations in the region unaddressed'. Kotelkin (note 3), p. 35.

[124] *Rossiyskaya Gazeta,* 17 Aug. 1995, p. 5, and 22 Apr. 1997, p. 7.

[125] Menon (note 21), p. 104.

[126] Ovchinnikov, V., 'Rossiya i Kitay: mnogopolyarny mir, spravedlivy mezhdunarodny poryadok' [Russia and China: a multipolar world, a just world order], *Rossiyskaya Gazeta,* 26 Apr. 1997, p. 3.

3. The management of Russian arms transfers

I. Introduction

During the Soviet period the decision-making prerogative in arms export policy belonged solely to the executive branch of government. The export of military equipment was a tightly controlled state monopoly of the Ministry of Foreign Economic Relations (MFER) in consultation with the Ministry of Defence (MOD) and the Ministry of Foreign Affairs (MOFA), although the MOFA appears to have played a secondary role. The Soviet defence industry ministries and arms producers do not appear to have had any major say and the legislature no voice at all in arms trade policy.

Since the emergence of the independent Russian state in December 1991, some new features have appeared in Russian decision making. However, it took some years to establish a more or less stable and effective system of arms transfer regulations in Russia. The decision-making system was transformed drastically in terms of both its structure and the principles on which it was based. In contrast with the absolute secrecy and dominance of the executive power under the Soviet regime, the Russian arms export policy was based on relative openness and some parliamentary control over arms transfers, in particular in the Duma's right of investigation. Russia abandoned its ideological approach to military–technical cooperation with foreign countries, and economic and strategic considerations became major factors in the shaping of its arms export policy.[1]

Along with many global developments, these changes facilitated military–technical cooperation between Russia and the East Asian countries. At the same time, lack of stability in the Russian arms export regulations and lack of coordination between the various gov-

---

[1] On the decision-making system of the USSR, see Kirshin, Yu., 'Conventional arms transfers during the Soviet period', ed. I. Anthony, SIPRI, *Russia and the Arms Trade* (Oxford University Press: Oxford, 1998), pp. 38–70. On the evolution of the Russian arms export decision-making system in the early 1990s, see Litavrin, P., 'The process of policy making and licensing for conventional arms transfers', ed. Anthony, pp. 107–16; and Sergounin, A. A. and Subbotin, S. V., 'In search of a new Russian arms export policy', *International Spectator* (Rome), no. 1 (1994), pp. 33–52. See also the SIPRI Internet site URL <http://www.sipri.se/projects/expcon/expcon.htm> for more recent information.

ernment bodies responsible for making and implementing arms transfer policy seriously hindered this cooperation. Both Russian defence industrialists and Russia's customers suffered from the negative consequences of the processes of the transitional period—the changing ground rules for cooperation, constant reorganizations of the organs responsible for the execution of deals, and problems of corruption and smuggling.

II. The decision-making system

The first new arms export decision-making system was introduced in Russia as of 2 January 1992. In contrast with the past, a mechanism for parliamentary control over arms exports was created. A special parliamentary group, the Special Commission on Military–Technical Cooperation (Spetsialnaya komissiya verkhovnogo soveta po voyenno-tekhnicheskomu sotrudnichestvu) was formed within the Supreme Soviet, responsible for supervising arms export activities and reporting to the Presidium of the Supreme Soviet on the annual plans for military–technical cooperation. Represented in the group were four permanent parliamentary committees and commissions for: (*a*) international affairs; (*b*) industry and power supply; (*c*) defence and security; and (*d*) planning, budget, taxation and pricing.[2]

A new system within the executive branch was established by presidential decree no. 507, 'On military–technical cooperation of the Russian Federation with foreign states', of 12 May 1992 (see figure 3.1).[3] The final decision on whether or not to provide military–technical assistance to a given country or group of countries rested solely with the Russian Government. The principal organization concerned with arms exports was the Interdepartmental Commission on Military–Technical Cooperation between the Russian Federation and Foreign Countries (Mezhvedomstvennaya komissiya po voyenno-tekhnicheskomu sotrudnichestvu Rossiyskoy Federatsii s inostrannymi gosudarstvami, KVTS), made up of the heads of the MFER, the

---

[2] *NATO's Sixteen Nations,* no. 6 (1992), p. 84; and Wulf, H. (ed.), SIPRI, *Arms Industry Limited* (Oxford University Press: Oxford, 1994), p. 134.

[3] 'Polozheniye o voyenno-tekhnicheskom sotrudnichestve Rossiyskoy Federatsii s zarubezhnymi stranami' [Regulations on military–technical cooperation between the Russian Federation and foreign countries], *Rossiyskaya Gazeta,* 16 May 1992; *NATO's Sixteen Nations,* no. 6 (1992), pp. 84–85; and *International Spectator* (Rome), vol. 28, no. 1 (Jan.–Mar. 1993), pp. 122–23.

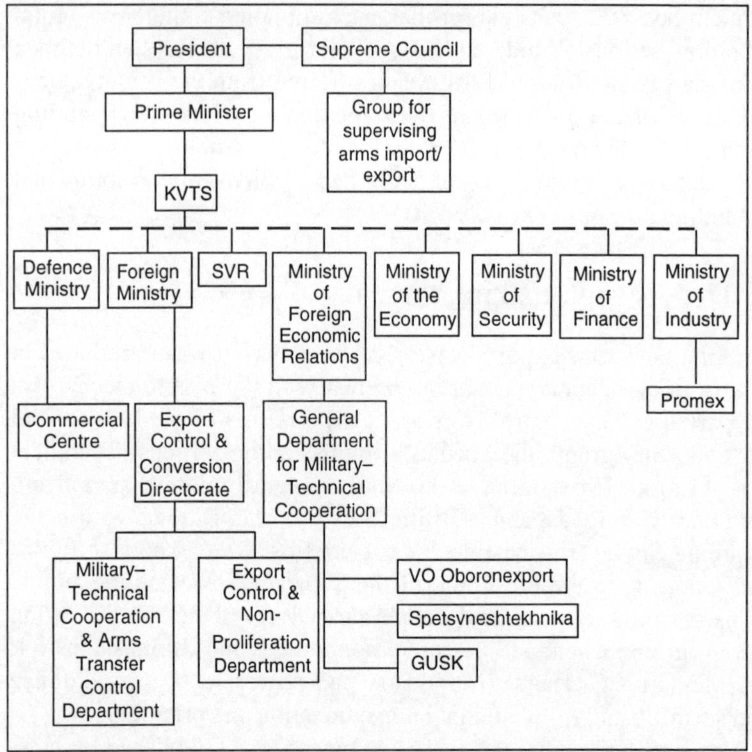

Figure 3.1. The Russian arms export decision-making system, 1992

SVR = Foreign Intelligence Service; GUSK = Central Directorate of Collaboration and Cooperation; KVTS = Interdepartmental Commission on Military–
Technical Cooperation between the Russian Federation and Foreign Countries.

Note: The broken line from the KVTS to the ministries indicates that the ministries are both represented on and subordinated to the KVTS.

MOFA, the Foreign Intelligence Service (Sluzhba Vneshney Raz-
vedki, SVR), the MOD, the Ministry of the Economy, the Ministry of
Industry, the Ministry of Finance and the Ministry of Security, and
nominally headed by the president. The KVTS considered all the
principal issues regarding deliveries of military *matériel* and on the
basis of its suggestions the government took its final decisions, which
were then forwarded to the organizations directly involved in export
operations. It was responsible not only for strategic decisions but also
for ensuring that inter-sectoral competition did not lower prices on the
international market. Its secretariat was made up of MFER officials.

Responsibility for the execution of exports was strictly controlled and rested solely with the foreign trade organizations of the MFER: Oboronexport (export of armaments and military *matériel*, ammunition and spare parts, and technical support); Spetsvneshtekhnika (technical assistance to customer countries in defence construction projects); and the Central Directorate of Collaboration and Cooperation (Glavnoye upravleniye po sotrudnichestvu i kooperatsii, GUSK, responsible for transferring licences for production of defence-related products and for delivery to these countries of equipment and materials needed in connection with licensing agreements or co-production programmes).[4] The activities of these three organizations were coordinated by a special unit of the MFER, the General Department for Military–Technical Cooperation.

Oboronexport was the leading body and the oldest arms exporter in the country, with 40 years of experience of military–technical cooperation and the reputation of a reliable, responsible partner with an efficient network of representatives. According to Major-General Sergey Karaoglanov, former Chairman of Oboronexport, its activities included: commercial and other operations on the export market for the delivery of defence-related products and services, including delivery through companies in foreign countries; technical assistance in training in, handling, use in combat, modernization and repair of armament and other defence *matériel*; mediation, consulting and other services related to foreign trade; and export–import of general-purpose products in the interest of other enterprises, associations and organizations of the Russian military–industrial complex.

The guiding principles of the activities of Oboronexport were described by Karaoglanov as being 'mutual benefit and . . . strict adherence to all the international agreements in the sphere of arms trading'.[5] The company tried to avoid the political aspects previously associated with defence exports, which implied that as a commercial enterprise it was looking for creditworthy customers, although traditional, less well-off partners were not to be let down. As Karaoglanov put it, 'Our policy as regards these customers is to look for compro-

---

[4] Decree no. 507 created the VO (Vneshnetorgovoye Obyedineniye, or export organization) Oboronexport from the Central Engineering Directorate (Glavnoye Inzhenernoye Upravleniye, GIU). Spetsvneshtekhnika was formed from the Central Technical Directorate (Glavnoye Tekhnicheskoye Upravleniye, GTU).

[5] *NATO's Sixteen Nations,* no. 6 (1992), p. 85.

mise solutions that solve the problems of financing in a way that is acceptable to both parties'.[6]

Apart from these agencies, Promex, the foreign trade organization operating in the Ministry of Industry's Directorate General for the Defence Industry, was involved in arms trading.[7] Furthermore, the Russian armed forces themselves became one of the biggest arms traders, selling excess weapons to foreign countries (including former Soviet republics involved in armed conflict with their neighbours).[8]

There were some serious differences of opinion regarding arms exports and controls within the government and parliament. Some experts and legislators suggested a liberalization of the export regime in order to give defence enterprises the opportunity to earn hard currency. Most top governmental officials favoured a state monopoly. Karaoglanov supported a compromise option:

Armament is a very peculiar and sensitive product. While free trade in, say, consumer goods would mainly affect the economic interests of this or that country, the same situation as regards arms would have a direct impact on the future of the whole of mankind. That is why, despite my complete adherence to the principles of market economy and manufacturer's freedom, I do believe that the trade in these specific goods should be centralised and concentrated in the hands of a foreign trade organisation (or a small number of them), under strict state control.[9]

At the same time, he recognized that it would be unnatural to cut manufacturing plants completely out of the process of selling their products, as had been done in the past, and that consideration must be given to their individual requirements in relation to a proper export control framework. As a result it was planned during these initial stages to grant manufacturing plants the right to select trade agents and marketing agencies from the limited circle of those authorized by the government, all of which could work together through all stages of the commercial process right up to the signature of the contract documents. The General Department for Military–Technical Cooperation was authorized to grant companies licences (called quotas) for production on the basis of contracts signed with foreign clients. At the

[6] *NATO's Sixteen Nations*, no. 6 (1992), p. 85.
[7] *International Spectator* (Rome), vol. 28, no. 1 (Jan.–Mar. 1993), p. 123.
[8] Anthony, I., 'Illict arms transfers', ed. Anthony (note 1), pp. 222–26.
[9] *NATO's Sixteen Nations*, no. 6 (1992), p. 85.

end of the production cycle, the company must again turn to the department for an export licence.[10]

This did not satisfy the arms producers. Their right to sell weapons through licences, granted by the Law on Conversion of the Defence Industry of 1992,[11] was being violated by the government. They were limited in the selection of trade agents, had no freedom at the operative levels of bargaining and delivery and, being dependent on mediators, could not get a fair share of the proceeds. This undermined their hopes of using earnings from arms exports for conversion, technological restructuring and the purchase of consumer goods.

The state monopoly was thus retained unchanged. Karaoglanov pointed out, for the benefit of Western businessmen, that 'presently not a single Russian organisation, with the exception of the three specialised foreign economic associations of the Ministry of Foreign Economic Relations, [has] been issued a general licence by the Russian Government for trading armament and combat *matériel*. Knowing this will help serious businessmen on some seemingly attractive offers'.[12] In another interview he said: 'All arms sales are controlled by the government. It is not possible for Russian factories to sell arms without us knowing'.[13]

Another delicate problem was the role of other executive agencies in arms trade policy. Their membership in the KVTS was to some extent only formal and could not resolve all the problems of coordination. The MOFA participated in the political evaluation of military cooperation with foreign countries, collected information on clients' needs through the embassies abroad and negotiated (by government assignment) general conditions of arms agreements. It had within its structure the Export Control and Conversion Directorate (Upravleniye po Kontrolyu za Eksportom i Konversii), including two specialized units—the Military–Technical Cooperation and Arms Transfer Control Department (Otdel po Voenno-Techicheskomu Sotrudnichestvu i

---

[10] *International Spectator* (Rome), vol. 28, no. 1 (Jan.–Mar. 1993), p. 123.

[11] Zakon Rossiyskoy Federatsii o konversii oboronnoy promyshlennosti v Rossiyskoy Federatsii [Russian Federation law on conversion of the defence industry in the Russian Federation], no. 2551-1, reproduced in *Rossiyskaya Gazeta,* 27 Apr. 1992. For an English translation, see US–Russia Business Development Committee, Defense Conversion Subcommittee, 'Russian Federation Law on Conversion of the Defense Industry in the Russian Federation', *Russian Defense Business Directory* (US Department of Commerce: Washington, DC, Nov. 1992), pp. 6–7.

[12] *NATO's Sixteen Nations*, no. 6 (1992), p. 86.

[13] *Jane's Defence Weekly,* 6 Feb. 1993, p. 32.

Kontrolyu za Eksportom Vooruzhenii) and the Export Control and Non-Proliferation Department (Otdel po Eksportnomu Kontrolyu i Nerasprostraneniyu).[14] However, their influence on the decision-making process was modest.

Under presidential decree no. 507, the SVR also had some responsibility for the arms trade: it was to 'collect and process information on questions of military–technical cooperation and help in checking the reliability of foreign partners'[15] and was responsible for drafting export contracts. It was not clear, however, how the SVR and the MFER coordinated their activities to avoid duplication.

The MOD was also engaged in the decision-making process. In accordance with decree no. 507 it was obliged to participate in the formulation of arms trade doctrine, to train foreign personnel and to assist in the exploitation of the military equipment sold.

On 2 January 1992 an all-Russian agency was established to manage the sale of Russian arms and war *matériel* to other members of the CIS and elsewhere. This agency, known as the Commercial Centre (Kommercheskiy Tsentr) and attached to the MOD, was permitted to keep revenues from arms sales to pay for welfare programmes for demobilized soldiers.[16]

The Ministry of the Economy together with the Ministry of Industry proposed the export list for the forthcoming year and the near future. The Ministry of Industry assessed and coordinated export offers of enterprises. All the above-mentioned ministries as well as the Ministry of Security and the State Customs Committee monitored the observance of the export control regulations and enforced arms embargoes.[17]

---

[14] *Russian Defense Business Directory* (note 11), p. 7-7.

[15] 'Polozheniye o voyenno-tekhnicheskom sotrudnichestve' (note 3), section 9.

[16] Anthony, I. *et al.*, 'The trade in major conventional weapons', *SIPRI Yearbook 1992: World Armaments and Disarmament* (Oxford University Press: Oxford, 1992), pp. 280–81.

[17] 'Polozheniye o voyenno-tekhnicheskom sotrudnichestve' (note 3); and 'Polozheniye o poryadke vvedeniya embargo na postavku vooruzheniya i voennoy tekhniki, okazaniye uslug voyenno-tekhnicheskogo kharaktera, a takzhe na postavku syrye, materialov, oborudovaniya i peredachu tekhnologii voyennogo i dvoiynogo naznacheniya zarubezhnym gosudarstvam, v tom chisle uchastnikam SNG' [Regulations on the procedure for imposing embargo on deliveries of armaments and military equipment, the provision of services of a military–technical nature, and on deliveries of raw and other materials and equipment and the transfer of military and dual-use technologies to foreign states, including the CIS members], presidential decree no. 235, 18 Feb. 1993, reproduced in *Rossiyskaya Gazeta*, 25 Feb. 1993; and *Sobranie aktov presidenta i pravitelstva Rossiyskoy Federatsii* [Collection of legislative acts of the President and Government of the Russian Federation], no. 8 (1993), pp. 799–800, English translation in Anthony (note 1), pp. 248–49.

The managerial problems under this decision-making system are: (*a*) the absence of a specific executive agency responsible for both the elaboration and the execution of arms trade policy; (*b*) lack of coordination between the different government bodies charged with the export of weapons; (*c*) duplication of functions and prerogatives; (*d*) a lack of long-term strategy and a predominance of commercial considerations (in contrast to the past); and (*e*) disputes with arms producers irritated by the monopolistic policies of the government. At the same time, there were some positive developments in arms trade policy decision making—for example, the 'de-ideologization' of arms transfer policy, openness (within reasonable limits), some parliamentary control and a weakening of the state monopoly.

After the 1993 parliamentary elections and the adoption of the new constitution in December, President Yeltsin decided to reorganize the decision-making system. The new constitution granted the president very broad powers, also in the fields of foreign policy and security. The president and the executive branch on the whole remained the main makers of arms export policy. The parliament (the State Duma and the Federation Council) was nearly isolated from decisions in this field, although some of its committees retained fairly modest supervision functions. For example, in April 1997 the Duma adopted a special resolution urging the executive power to tighten its control on the activities of various government bodies in the field of military–technical cooperation with foreign countries.[18] The resolution was provoked by the investigation of the Defence Committee, led by Lev Rokhlin, on illegal arms transfers to Armenia, first disclosed by Aman Tuleyev, Minister for Cooperation with CIS Member States (Minsotrudnichestva).[19] In 1997–98 the Duma discussed a bill on arms export control regulation which was to establish a procedure for parliamentary control over arms transfer policy. For various reasons it has not been adopted.

As with other areas of foreign and military policy, the president was at the top of the new executive branch decision-making pyramid. At that time, his assistant for military–technical cooperation with foreign

---

[18] 'O merakh po soblyudeniyu zakonodatelstva Rossiyskoy Federatsii pri postavkakh vooruzheniya i voyennoy tekhniki inostrannym gosudarstvam' [On measures to enforce the legislation of the Russian Federation in the process of arms and military equipment transfers to foreign states], resolution no. 1316-II, 11 Apr. 1997, reproduced in *Rossiyskaya Gazeta*, 22 Apr. 1997, p. 6.

[19] Anthony, I., 'Introduction', ed. Anthony (note 1), p. 13; and *Jane's Defence Weekly*, 19 Mar. 1997, p. 16.

countries, Boris Kuzyk, was responsible for handling routine matters and represented presidential interests at various levels of the government hierarchy. The president personally controlled the government bodies involved in arms transfers. According to Kuzyk, Yeltsin's personal intervention was very helpful in overcoming numerous bureaucratic barriers: 'He supported our initiative and his direct assistance allowed us to sign at least 10 major contracts with states which had not been our traditional clients'.[20]

Under presidential decree no. 2251 of 30 December 1994, the State Committee on Military–Technical Policy (Gosudarstvenny komitet voyenno-tekhnicheskoy politike, GKVTP) was established and given principal authority over arms export questions within the executive power (see figure 3.2).[21] It considered all the principal issues on deliveries of military *matériel*, and its decisions were the basis for the export operations of other government bodies. The GKVTP was not only responsible for strategic decisions but also examined more technical issues, such as licensing, and tried to ensure that inter-sectoral competition did not lower prices on the international market. Its chairman had the rank of minister. It was subordinated directly to the president but First Deputy Prime Minister Oleg N. Soskovets was charged with day-to-day control over the GKVTP. It had 243 staff, of whom about 95 were assigned from the MOD, the president's security service, the Federal Counter-Intelligence Service (Federalnaya Sluzhba Kontrrazvedki, later renamed the Federal Security Service, Federalnaya Sluzhba Bezopasnosti) and the SVR. The General Department for Military–Technical Cooperation and its personnel were transferred from the MFER to the GKVTP.[22]

Under government decree no. 879 of 4 September 1995, besides the GKVTP, the MOD and the State Committee on Defence Industries (Goskomoboronprom) also had to be involved in the issuing of export–import licences.[23] The MOD evaluated applications from the

<hr>

[20] Cited in Perera, J., 'Russia's arms sales increasing', *Jane's Intelligence Review and Jane's Sentinel Pointer*, Jan. 1997, p. 2.

[21] 'O Gosudarstvennom komitete Rossiyskoy Federatsii po voyenno-tekhnicheskoy politike' [On the State Committee of the Russian Federation on Military–Technical Policy], reproduced in *Rossiyskaya Gazeta,* 10 Jan. 1995, p. 4.

[22] 'O Gosudarstvennom komitete Rossiyskoy Federatsii po voyenno-tekhnicheskoy politike' (note 21).

[23] 'Polozheniye o poryadke litsenzirovaniya v Rossiyskoy Federatsii eksporta i importa produktsii, rabot i uslug voyennogo naznacheniya' [Regulations on the procedure for licensing export and import of military products, works and services in the Russian Federation], *Kommersant*, 10 Oct. 1995, pp. 68–69; and [Regulations on the procedure for licensing

technical point of view and Goskomoboronprom provided the GKVTP with information on the legal status of applicants. Licences were issued for 12-month periods.

The Interdepartmental Coordinating Council for Military–Technical Policy (Koordinirovanny mezhduvedomstvenny sovet po voyenno-tekhnicheskoy politike, KMSVTP), which replaced the KVTS, was a subsidiary body created by presidential decree no. 590 of 14 June 1995 and charged with more general oversight of arms transfer policy and arbitration of inter-agency disputes.[24] The MFER, the MOFA, the SVR, the MOD, the Ministry of the Economy, Goskomoboronprom, the Ministry of Finance, the State Property Control Committee, the State Customs Committee and the Federal Counter-Intelligence Service were all represented on the KMSVTP.

Rosvooruzheniye, the State Corporation for Trade in Armaments and Military Technical Cooperation, established in November 1993, was an implementation agency which played a central role in negotiating and carrying out arms export deals. Under presidential decree no. 1008 of 5 October 1995, it was the main government instrument for arms export–import operations.[25] However, a limited number of state-owned and private trading companies and defence plants were

export and import of military-purpose products, work and services in the Russian Federation], *Sobranie zakonodatelstva Rossiyskoy Federatsii* [Collection of legislative acts of the Russian Federation], no. 37 (1995), pp. 6789–94 (article 3626), English translation in Anthony (note 1), pp. 256–59.

[24] 'O Koordinatsioonnom mezhvedomstvennom sovete po voenno-technicheskoy politike Rossiyskoi Federatsii [On the Interdepartmental Coordinating Council for Military-Technical Policy of the Russian Federation], *Sobranie zakonodatelstva Rossiyskoy Federatsii* [Collection of legislative acts of the Russian Federation], no. 25 (1995), p. 4519 (article 2379); and 'Polozheniye o Koordinatsioonnom mezhvedomstvennom sovete po voenno-technicheskoy politike Rossiyskoi Federatsii' [Regulations on the Interdepartmental Coordinating Council for Military–Technical Policy of the Russian Federation], *Sobranie zakonodatelstva Rossiyskoy Federatsii*, no. 25 (1995), pp. 4519–23 (article 2379), English translation in Anthony (note 1), pp. 243–46.

[25] 'O voyenno-tekhnicheskom sotrudnichestve Rossiyskoy Federatsii s zarubezhnymi stranami' [On military–technical cooperation between the Russian Federation and foreign countries], reproduced in *Rossiyskaya Gazeta*, 17 Oct. 1995; and Decree of the President of the Russian Federation on military–technical cooperation of the Russian Federation with foreign countries (basic provisions) and Regulations on military–technical cooperation of the Russian Federation with foreign states, approved by the Decree of the President of the Russian Federation of 5 Oct. 1995, no. 1008, *Sobranie zakonodatelstva Rossiyskoy Federatsii* [Collection of legislative acts of the Russian Federation], no. 41 (1995), pp. 7203–11 (article 3876). The decree and regulations are reproduced in English in Anthony (note 1), pp. 238–43.

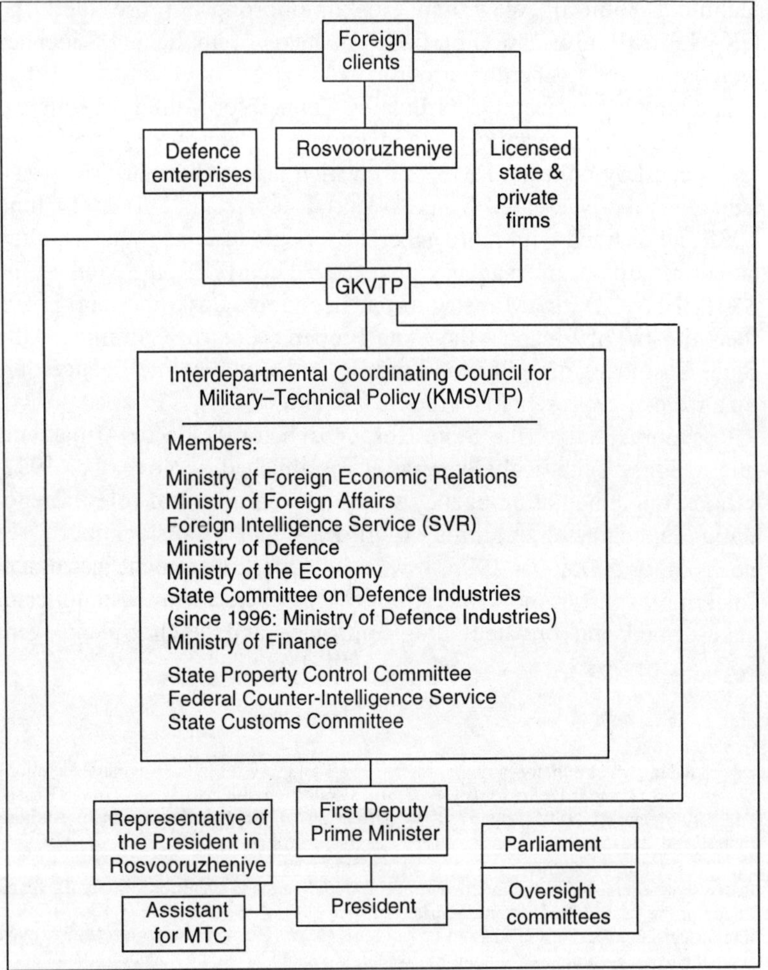

Figure 3.2. The Russian arms export decision-making system, 1994

GKVTP = State Committee on Military–Technical Policy; MTC = Military–Technical Cooperation.

also granted licences to carry out foreign trade in military equipment by government decree no. 479 of 6 May 1994.[26]

---

[26] 'O predostavlenii predpriyatiyam prava uchastiya v voyenno-tekhnicheskom sotrudnichestve Rossiyskoy Federatsii s zarubezhnymi stranami' [On granting enterprises the right to participate in military–technical cooperation between the Russian Federation and foreign countries], *Sobranie Zakonodatelstva Rossiyskoy Federatsii* [Collection of legislative acts of

While Rosvooruzheniye was created to stop uncoordinated activities on the part of individual plants and companies, in the short term its creation added to the confusion. Deals then in progress or being finalized by individual enterprises were suddenly disrupted by a change of the ground rules.

On 4 March 1994 President Yeltsin issued decree no. 450 to establish the post of his representative in Rosvooruzheniye.[27] His main functions were to protect the state's interests in the company, to supervise and audit Rosvooruzheniye's activities, to coordinate arms sales policies, and to make suggestions on future policies for the president. The representative has ministerial rank.

Despite the central role Rosvooruzheniye has played in both negotiating and carrying out arms export deals, its monopoly has sometimes been challenged by other state bodies involved in foreign economic relations. Some deals have been delayed by customs. In early 1997 the veterinary border service prohibited a shipment of Chinese pork paid for with Russian weapons on a barter basis.[28] It was very difficult for Rosvooruzheniye to resolve the conflict.

At the same time, with the assistance of the GKVTP, Rosvooruzheniye succeeded in its bureaucratic war against the rival arms trading companies. By presidential decree no. 1008 most of the licences that had been granted were cancelled or put under consideration by the GKVTP.[29] New arms export regulations were issued by the

the Russian Federation], no. 4 (1994), p. 557 (article 364). See also 'Polozheniye o sertifikatsii i registratsii predpriyatii, obladayushchikh pravom eksporta vooruzhenii, voyennogo snaryazheniya, a takzhe rabot i uslug voyennogo naznacheniya [Regulations on the certification and registering of enterprises for the right to export armaments, military equipment and military-purpose work and services], *Sobranie Zakonodatelstva Rossiyskoy Federatsii*, no. 4 (1994), pp. 557–63. Both are reproduced in English in Anthony (note 1), pp. 252–55.

[27] 'Dekret Prezidenta Rossiyskoy Federatsii ob utverzhdenii polozheniya o predstavitele Prezidenta Rossiyskoy Federatsii v gosudarstvennoy kompanii Rosvooruzheniye' [Decree of the President of the Russian Federation approving the regulations on the status of the representative of the President of the Russian Federation in the state company Rosvooruzheniye], no. 450, 4 Mar. 1994; and 'Polozheniye o predstavitele Prezidenta Rossiyskoy Federatsii v gosudarstvennoy kompanii Rosvooruzheniye' [Regulations on the representative of the President of the Russian Federation in the state company Rosvooruzheniye], approved by decree no. 450, 4 Mar. 1994, *Sobranie aktov prezidenta i pravitelstva Rossiyskoy Federatsii* [Collection of legislative acts of the President and Government of the Russian Federation], no. 10 (1994), pp. 880–83 (article 778), English translation in Anthony (note 1), pp. 246–48.

[28] Platkovsky, A., 'Oruzheyny biznes na grani myasnoy voiny' [Weapon business on the brink of the pork war], *Izvestiya*, 15 Mar. 1997.

[29] 'O voyenno-tekhnicheskom sotrudnichestve Rossiyskoy Federatsii s zarubezhnymi stranami' (note 25).

government on 4 September 1995.[30] Only MiG-MAPO was allowed to act more or less independently in the foreign markets.

However, the government soon found itself under powerful attack from Goskomoboronprom, which emphasized the critical condition most defence plants were in. Reacting to lobbying by the military–industrial complex, on 19 February 1996 the government issued executive orders nos. 202–208 by which seven more companies were granted export licences (Antey, Gidromash, Izhmash, Metrovagonmash, Rosvertol, the Tula Instrument Making Design Bureau and the Ufimskoye Engine-Building Industrial Association).[31] By 1997 some 15 defence enterprises had been granted the right to sell their output on the world markets independently, but the only one which has had notable success is MAPO.[32]

In August 1996 the entire arms export decision-making system was reshuffled again. By presidential decree no. 686 of 8 May 1996, Goskomoboronprom was transformed into Minoboronprom (the Ministry of Defence Industry). The post of assistant to the president on military–technical cooperation was abolished. The position of presidential representative in Rosvooruzheniye was vacant for several months.[33] The GKVTP was abolished in August 1996 by presidential decree no. 1177 and its functions were transferred back to the MFER.[34] Minoboronprom was abolished in March 1997 and its functions in the sphere of military–technical policy transferred to the Ministry of the Economy. Some experts, however, questioned the ministry's capability to handle arms export business because of its cumbersome bureaucratic structure.[35]

A special statute on the Ministry of Foreign Economic Relations and Commerce (MFERC) was adopted by government decree no. 402

[30] 'Polozheniye o poryadke litsenzirovaniya v Rossiyskoy Federatsii eksporta i importa produktsii, rabot i uslug voyennogo naznacheniya' (note 23), pp. 68–69.

[31] English translations in Anthony (note 1), pp. 263–68.

[32] Perera (note 20), p. 2.

[33] Pappe, Y., 'Otraslevye lobbi v pravitelstve Rossii' [Sectoral lobbies in the Russian Government], *Pro et Contra*, autumn 1996, p. 73.

[34] 'O strukture federalnykh organov ispolnitelnoy vlasti' [On the structure of the federal bodies of executive power], presidential decree no. 1177, 14 Aug. 1996, *Sobranie zakonodatelstva Rossiyskoy Federatsii* [Collection of legislative acts of the Russian Federation], no. 34 (1996), p. 4082; and Executive order no. 133, 4 Feb. 1997, reproduced in *Rossiyskaya Gazeta*, 20 Feb. 1997.

[35] Rybas, A., 'Opasnaya tendentsiya' [Dangerous trend], *Nezavisimoye Voyennoye Obozreniye*, 12–19 Feb. 1998, p. 6.

of 7 April 1997 (see figure 3.3).[36] Along with internal commerce and international trade, the MFERC is responsible for military–technical cooperation with foreign countries.

Its functions and powers are much broader than those of the former GKVTP and include the drafting (together with other executive bodies) of legislation and executive orders on military–technical policy and annual programmes of military–technical cooperation with foreign countries; the coordination of the activities of other government agencies in this field; preparation of conceptual approaches to military–technical policy and analyses of the results of Russia's arms export policies; proposing the export-oriented items of the state defence order, including the budgetary mechanism; control over prices of military products and services; and the issuing of export–import licences.[37] The MFERC seems to have assumed not only the powers of the GKVTP but also partly those of Minoboronprom, the MOD and the secret services. In fact, the 1992–93 decision-making system was restored (except for the existence of Rosvooruzheniye). However, the new system was much more centralized than the old one: there are few arms trading firms, and they have only limited powers.

In August 1997 the political pendulum swung again. At least two factors—scandals involving former leaders of Rosvooruzheniye, the GKVTP and some officials from the president's administration, and the dissatisfaction of arms producers with the highly centralized arms export system—forced the Kremlin to reorganize the decision-making mechanism. On 20 August 1997 Yeltsin signed decree no. 907 'On measures to strengthen state control of foreign trade activity in the field of military–technical cooperation of the Russian Federation with foreign states' (see figure 3.4).[38] The KMSVTP was reorganized into the Interdepartmental Coordinating Council on Military–Technical Cooperation between the Russian Federation and Foreign States

---

[36] 'Polozheniye o Ministerstve vneshnikh ekonomicheskikh svyazey i torgovli Rossiyskoy Federatsii' [Decree of the Government of the Russian Federation approving the Statute on the Ministry of Foreign Economic Relations and Trade of the Russian Federation], reproduced in *Rossiyskaya Gazeta,* 22 Apr. 1997, p. 5, English translation in Anthony (note 1), pp. 270–78.

[37] *Rossiyskaya Gazeta,* 22 Apr. 1997 (note 36), p. 5.

[38] 'O merakh po usileniyu gosudarstvennogo kontrolya vneshnetorgovoy deyatelnosti v sfere voenno-tekhnicheskogo sotrudnichestva Rossiyskoy Federatsii s inostrannymi gosudarstvami' [On measures to strengthen state control of foreign trade activity in the field of military–technical cooperation of the Russian Federation with foreign states], *Rossiyskaya Gazeta,* 22 Aug. 1997, p. 11, English translation in Anthony (note 1), pp. 279–81.

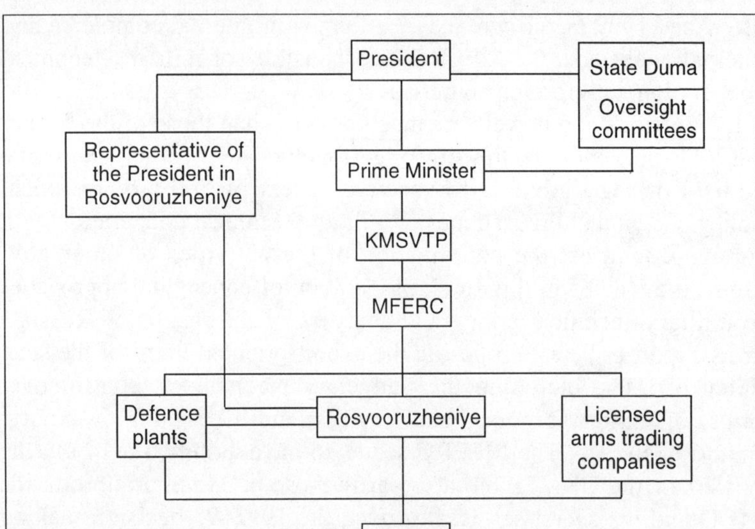

Figure 3.3. The Russian arms export decision-making system, April 1997

KMSVTP = Interdepartmental Coordinating Council for Military–Technical Policy; MFERC = Ministry of Foreign Economic Relations and Commerce.

(Koordinatsionniy mezhvedomstvenny sovet po voenno-tekhnicheskomu sotrudnichestvu Rossiyskoy Federatsii s inostrannymi gosudarstvami, KMS).

The KMS is charged with several responsibilities: defining priorities in military–technical cooperation with foreign states; proposing international agreements on matters of military–technical cooperation; monitoring the implementation of such cooperation with foreign powers; determining which military-purpose products can be permitted to be transferred to foreign customers; drawing up a list of states to be allowed to take delivery of military-purpose products; granting Russian organizations the right to engage in the arms trade and stripping them of this right; coordinating the activities of the federal executive bodies in the field of military–technical cooperation; organizing and holding exhibitions of arms and *matériel*; and deciding the composition and procedure of supervisory commissions to monitor the activities and financial status of state intermediaries—federal state companies engaged in arms export activities.[39] The KMS is composed of representatives of the main foreign policy and defence agencies and chaired by the Prime Minister. Real power is concentrated in the hands of its Deputy Chairman, Yakov M. Urinson, Deputy Chairman of the Russian Government and Minister of the Economy.

Although the MFERC had two seats in the KMS (for the minister and deputy minister) and the latter became the council's executive secretary, its powers were limited. Its prerogatives in fields such as the issuing of export–import licences, the drafting of legislation and international agreements, and the defining of priorities were undermined by the requirement to coordinate its activities with the KMS. Responsibility for relations with arms producers, price policies and the budget process were taken over by the Ministry of the Economy. The MFER in fact became a bureaucratic 'rubber stamp' rather than a policy-making body.

Moreover, the system of implementation of arms export decisions has been decentralized. Instead of the single state intermediary—Rosvooruzheniye—three companies were created—Rosvooruzheniye, which retained its former functions; Promexport, which was to export surplus arms and military hardware from the inventory of the Russian armed forces and of spare parts, components and service support; and Rossiyskiye Tekhnologii (Russian Technologies), specialized in military technology transfers.[40] In addition, on 25 February 1998 then Prime Minister Viktor Chernomyrdin approved the statute on the register of organizations which have the right to conduct foreign trade in products with military applications.[41] By May 1998, 15 defence enterprises had been granted arms export licences.[42]

---

[39] 'Polozheniye o Koordinatsionnom mezhvedomstvennom sovete po voenno-tekhnicheskomu sotrudnichestvu Rossiyskoy Federatsii s inostrannymi gosudarstvami' [Statute of the Interdepartmental Coordinating Council on Military–Technical Cooperation between the Russian Federation and foreign states], *Rossiyskaya Gazeta*, 26 Aug. 1997, English translation in Anthony (note 1), pp. 282–84.

[40] 'O merakh po usileniyu gosudarstvennogo kontrolya' (note 38), p. 11. See also 'Ustav federalnogo gosudarstvennogo unitarnogo predpriyatiya Gosudarstvennaya kompaniya Rosvooruzheniye' [Statute on the Federal State Unitary Enterprise the State Company Rosvooruzheniye], Decree of the Chairman of the Government of the Russian Federation no. 1658 (31 Dec. 1997); and 'Ustav federalnogo gosudarstvennogo unitarnogo predpriyatiya Promexport' [Statute on the Federal State Unitary Enterprise Promexport], *Rossiyskaya Gazeta*, 31 Jan. 1998, p. 5.

[41] *Nezavisimoye Voyennoye Obozreniye*, 6–12 Mar. 1998, p. 3.

[42] Klenov, V., 'Slukhi o smerti "oboronki", pokhozhe, silno preuvelicheny' [It appears that rumours of the defence industry's death are strongly exaggerated], *Rossiyskaya Gazeta*, 30 Apr. 1998, p. 10.

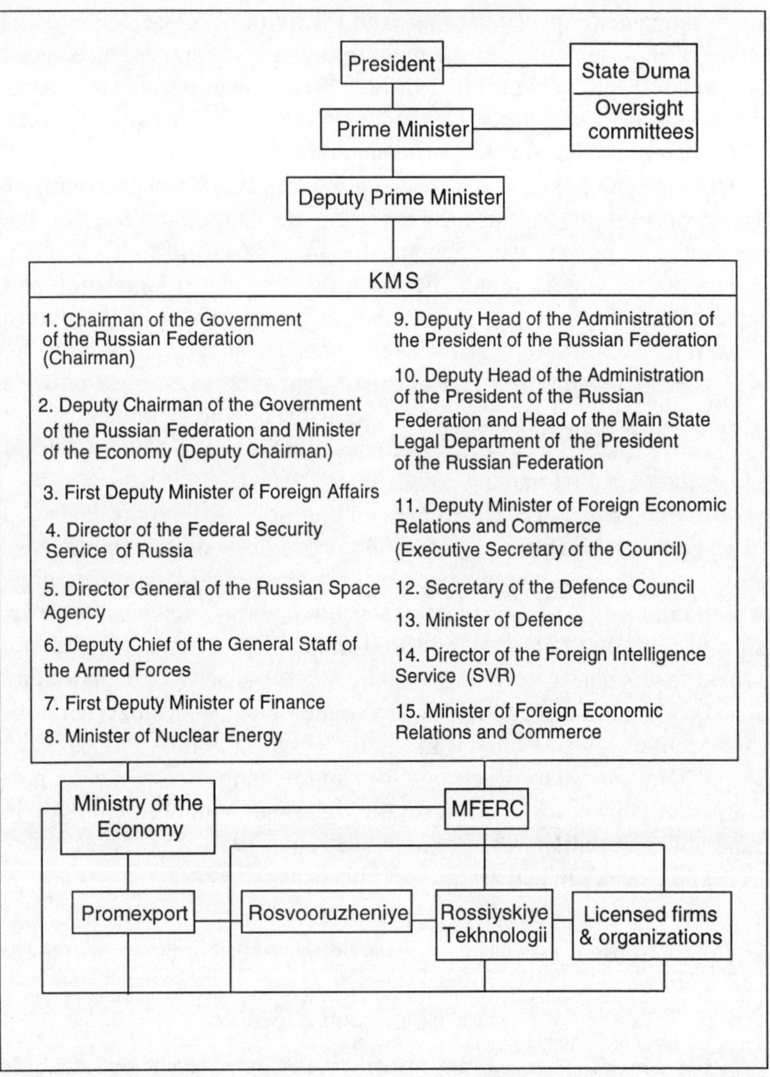

Figure 3.4. The Russian arms export decision-making system, August 1997

KMS = Interdepartmental Coordinating Council on Military–Technical Cooperation between the Russian Federation and Foreign States; MFERC = Ministry of Foreign Economic Relations and Commerce.

The reform of the decision-making mechanism had both positive and negative results. It created a more favourable atmosphere for arms producers as regards their access to international markets. It also tightened government control over the financial aspects of arms trade firms' activities, the lack of which had previously made illicit financial operations and corruption easy. However, despite the intention of the president to strengthen control over arms transfer policy, the new system lacks efficient leadership and coordination. There is no single body, such as the GKVTP, which is responsible for both decision-making and policy implementation.

Because of its composition the KMS could easily become hostage to the bureaucratic warfare between the MFERC, the Ministry of the Economy, the MOD, the MOFA, and so on. As a result of that warfare, in early 1998 Yakov Urinson was replaced by Chernomyrdin as the person chiefly responsible for arms export policy.[43] Many Russian experts stress that the decentralization of the arms export system could once again result in new inconsistencies, corruption, scandals and abuses.[44] Some components of the reform have proved to be hasty and unrealistic. For example, the setting up of Rossiyskiye Tekhnologii has been postponed because of the lack of finance, personnel and a clear business concept.

III. Arms deals with countries in East Asia

From 1991 first Oboronexport and the Central Engineering Directorate (Glavnoye inzhenernoye upravleniye, GIU, within the MFER) and then Rosvooruzheniye were the chief negotiators for major arms deals involving East Asian countries. Requests for Russian military equipment and related technology were usually relayed to these agencies through the MOFA and the MFER. Applications were first considered by the licensing authority (the KVTS or the GKVTP). Afterwards the state handling authority (Rosvooruzheniye) defined specific defence plants which might be interested in producing or exporting the arms which had been licensed in collaboration with Goskomoboronprom and the MOD. If an enterprise was the only producer of a given system the choice was easy: for example, the Krasnoye Sormovo plant in Nizhniy Novgorod was the principal producer of the Kilo (Varshav-

---

⁴³ Rybas (note 35), p. 6.
⁴⁴ Rybas (note 35), p. 6.

yanka) Class submarine and the Irkutsk Aircraft Production Association (IAPO) was the main builder of the Su-27 (Flanker) fighter aircraft. If a deal could involve several exporters Rosvooruzheniye was subjected to intensive lobbying by arms producers. For example, MiG-29 fighter aircraft which were sold to Malaysia and offered to China could have been transferred by either MiG-MAPO or the Sokol plant in Nizhniy Novgorod.

Orders were sometimes given to the plant which was in the worst economic situation and sometimes to the one able to produce the best equipment. In the case of orders by China, equipment was usually taken 'off the shelf' from unpaid production undertaken for the Russian MOD or a foreign customer. According to Nikolay Zharkov, Director of the Krasnoye Sormovo plant, two Kilo Class submarines that were sold to China were initially designated for Poland and Romania, which had refused to pay for them at the last moment.[45] According to unconfirmed reports, 50 T-80 tanks were sold to China by the Kirov Plant in St Petersburg after the Russian MOD refused to pay for them.[46] Production of two Sovremenny Class destroyers was started by the St Petersburg North Yard for the Russian Navy and finished for China with only some modifications. However, a third and a fourth Kilo submarine were produced specially for the Chinese Navy.[47]

After a decision on the exporter was taken, Rosvooruzheniye formed a mixed team involving its officials and representatives of the producer to negotiate price and payment schedules with the client. The representatives of the enterprises had no major voice in the negotiating process, usually playing more the role of consultants. On a number of occasions negotiations were carried out only by the state agency. For example, the Kilo submarine deal (including the setting of prices and other financial conditions) was concluded by Rosvooruzheniye with little participation of the Krasnoye Sormovo plant.[48] An enterprise might, however, have some opportunity to renegotiate technical aspects of the contract (such as the delivery and payment schedule or the shares of hard currency and barter payments): Zharkov succeeded in increasing the hard-currency element of

---

[45] *Izvestiya,* 10 Sep. 1994, p. 3.

[46] *Izvestiya,* 30 Mar. 1994, p. 4.

[47] On the Kilo Class submarine sale and other arms sales to China, see chapter 4 in this volume.

[48] *Delo,* 24–30 Mar. 1995, p. 7.

the submarine deal through direct negotiations with China after the general contract had been signed.[49] The producer was also responsible for adapting the weapon system to the specific requirements of the Chinese armed forces and for after-sales service.

Regional governments also had some voice in arms export decisions (e.g., those of Irkutsk, Nizhniy Novgorod, St Petersburg, Tula and Yekaterinburg promoted the establishment of arms trading firms and the issue of export licences for defence plants), and local governments received foreign delegations to assure them of their interest in and support for the Russian defence industry. By May 1998 Rosvooruzheniye had 10 regional divisions helping defence plants and local governments to find foreign partners.[50]

IV. Management: production and finance

The management of the production process for arms transfers depended on the conditions laid down in the contract. The producers managed the programmes themselves, including coordination of the many levels of production and suppliers of equipment and sub-systems (e.g., more than 200 enterprises were engaged in a Sino-Russian co-production programme to produce the Su-27 fighter).[51] This represents a fundamental change. After 1993 many defence enterprises became joint-stock companies, largely independent of the central government.[52] Plants applied for local and central government support only when they had trouble with subcontractors.

Some problems can be identified in the design bureau–production enterprise relationship. A number of design bureaux complained about neglect of their copyright for particular weapon systems. In most cases designers and manufacturers have moved to form production associations that will ensure that they both receive a share of the proceeds from sales of a given weapon system. For example, the Krasnoye Sormovo plant works in close contact with its design bureau in St Petersburg. In 1994–95 it used the facilities of the bureau

---

[49] *Delo,* 24–30 Mar. 1995, p. 7.

[50] Klenov (note 42), p. 10; and *Rossiyskaya Gazeta,* 13 Jan. 1998, p. 2.

[51] Kotelkin, A., 'Russia and the world arms market', *International Affairs* (Moscow), vol. 42, no. 4 (1996), p. 35. See also chapter 4 in this volume.

[52] By Apr. 1995, 22.5% of shares of the Krasnoye Sormovo plant had been sold at auction and 35% more were to be auctioned. *Delo,* 7–13 Apr. 1995, p. 3. In July 1995 the Sokol plant also sold 22% of its shares at auction. *Birzha,* 14 July 1995, p. 4.

to test submarines in the open sea before they were transferred to China.[53] The MiG Design Bureau agreed to sign final contracts together with the assembly plants of MAPO and Rosvooruzheniye. This triple signature is also intended to reassure the potential customer that the Russian Government is in full control of the deal. The general designer will be responsible for aircraft modifications, while the director of the assembly facility will be responsible for maintenance, technical service and timely supply of spare parts.[54]

The formation of financial–industrial groups became an important instrument for the survival of the military–industrial complex in the transition period, and the defence industry is also using them to develop its export activities. For example, in early 1996 the St Petersburg-based Admiralty Shipyard and Inkombank, a leading commercial bank in Russia, established a financial–industrial group to improve the competitiveness of the Kilo Class submarine on the international market.[55]

V. Management: problems and solutions

A number of complaints have been lodged against Rosvooruzheniye and other government agencies by industrialists and arms trading companies, many about the way in which they handle their business. In particular, they blame Rosvooruzheniye for neglecting the economic interests of the producers.

The financial conditions of arms deals with East Asian countries are an unresolved problem. China usually pays in hard currency for only 20–30 per cent of the contract value; the rest consists of shipments of consumer goods. For example, Russia received hard-currency payments to cover one-third of the value of the first Su-27 aircraft contract (1992) and 35 per cent of a deal involving 77-mm calibre shipborne guns produced by the Mashzavod Machine Building Plant in Nizhniy Novgorod.[56] The Novgorod industrial and trading association signed a contract with the authorities of the southern Chinese province of Hainan for delivery of 212 railway wagonloads of mango

[53] *Delo,* 7–13 Apr. 1995, p. 3.

[54] Kogan, E., 'The Russian defence industry: trends, difficulties and obstacles', *Asian Defence Journal,* Oct. 1994, p. 45.

[55] *Jane's Intelligence Review and Jane's Sentinel Pointer,* Oct. 1996, p. 1.

[56] *Delo,* 24–30 Mar. 1995, p. 7; *Birzha,* 14 Apr. 1995, p. 3; *Far Eastern Economic Review,* 3 Sep. 1992, p. 21; and *Jane's Defence Weekly,* 6 Feb. 1993, p. 32.

juice in exchange for an Il-76 transport aircraft. About a quarter of Malaysia's $550 million order for MiG-29 aircraft was paid for in palm oil.[57] Some newspapers reported that the Philippines was interested in buying arms from Russia and offered bananas in exchange.[58]

Russia has sometimes succeeded in signing more advantageous contracts. For example, in the deal to transfer the Kilo Class submarine to China, the producer was able to shift the ratio of hard currency to barter to 50 : 50. However, the Krasnoye Sormovo plant remained dissatisfied. After paying taxes and commissions, its hard-currency payment was only 8–10 per cent of the value of the contract.[59]

The consumer goods received in partial payment are not popular in Russia because of their low quality and because they are available elsewhere. Lack of clarity in the contracts has been used by some of Russia's partners (particularly by China) to propose an assortment of goods that left no choice for the Russian counterparts. These goods could not be effectively resold in Russia or re-exported by the arms-producing plants. At present, the Russian defence industry still has no alternative to such business practices. Industrial leaders are very critical of what they call the 'banana approach' (referring to the Philippines' proposal) and are putting pressure on the Russian Government and Rosvooruzheniye to modify the approach to contracts. In their view this kind of financing can serve only as a temporary tactic to survive a transitional period.

By some accounts, in November 1996 China and Russia agreed that all future arms transactions would be fully paid for in hard currency.[60] However, recent reports, including those on their April 1997 summit meeting, do not confirm this: China and Russia still have differences of opinion as to the method of payment.[61] Even if they do move to a purely hard-currency basis, it is improbable that Russia will succeed in concluding similar agreements with other East Asian countries.

As a state company Rosvooruzheniye often established the prices and financial conditions of agreements on the basis of political and strategic rather than commercial considerations. This was similar to

[57] Hull, A. and Markov, D., 'Trends in the arms market', *Jane's Intelligence Review*, May 1997, p. 234.

[58] *Moscow News,* 19 Mar. 1993, p. 5.

[59] *Delo,* 24–30 Mar. 1995, p. 7.

[60] *Jane's Defence Weekly,* 15 Jan. 1997, p. 5.

[61] Litovkin, V., 'Kitayskaya armiya krepchayet russkim oruzhiem' [The Chinese Army is getting stronger due to Russian arms], *Izvestiya,* 25 Apr. 1997.

Soviet practice. For instance, Kilo Class submarines were sold at sub-stantially reduced prices for that class of vessels—$90 million each—while Germany is believed to have sold submarines for $200 million each in 1994.[62]

Furthermore, industrialists were unhappy with the size of the commission charged by Rosvooruzheniye for its services. Under the 1997 legislation, Rosvooruzheniye was allowed to take about 5–10 per cent of the value of sales in commission. The rest of the after-tax proceeds should, theoretically, go to the producers. In reality the commission was often 15–20 per cent. In the case of the T-80 tank deal it was 25 per cent.[63] Other government and private trading companies limited themselves to commissions of up to 5 per cent. This practice often led to corruption in Rosvooruzheniye. An investigation in 1996 revealed that it was paying middlemen a 20 per cent commission on all trades and that these commissions totalled $30–35 million in 1994. In another case, Russian officials received $75 000 in bribes to issue export certificates.[64]

While deals with many East Asian countries were usually concluded on the basis of barter, Rosvooruzheniye took all its commission in hard currency regardless of the conditions of the contract. Naturally, this provoked resentment in the enterprises which were left with proceeds in barter form. Moreover, plants which succeeded in getting some part of their payments in hard currency were required, under the prevailing rules, to sell 50 per cent of the currency earned to the Central Bank of Russia at an artificial exchange rate.

Russian industrialists also insist that a general arms export contract should be signed after or at least simultaneously with an agreement on the method of payment. This could increase the bargaining power of Russia both in deciding the hard-currency portion of a deal and in the selection of consumer goods accepted as barter.

The actors in the arms trade have been disappointed with the terms of consideration and the processing of applications from foreign clients established in August 1997. The waiting period for applications for spare parts has been extended from 3–6 to 6–12 months and that for finished military products from 8–12 to 12–18 months.[65] Under these circumstances, emergency military assistance has become

[62] *Izvestiya,* 10 Sep. 1994, p. 3.
[63] *Izvestiya,* 30 Mar. 1994, p. 4.
[64] Hull and Markov, 'Trends in the arms market' (note 57), p. 236.
[65] Rybas (note 35), p. 6.

nearly impossible. Arms producers fear that this can undermine Russia's reputation on the world markets.

Defence plants are discontented with the way the government selected the banks to be authorized to handle the financial operations of Rosvooruzheniye. According to one report, a banker offered a $250 million bribe to a government official to use his bank for Chinese payments for Russian arms. The same report identifies General Alexander Korzhakov, former head of the president's security service, as a driving force behind a secret presidential decree appointing 10 commercial banks (Uneximbank, Inkombank, Tokobank, Vneshekonombank, Vneshtorgbank, Mezhkombank, Menatep, Eurofinance, the Moscow National Bank and the National Reserve Bank) as authorized state agents for Rosvooruzheniye.[66] In reality, the use of these banks led to numerous abuses in the system of payment. Proceeds from arms deals often disappeared in secret bank accounts in foreign countries and were spent on bribes and on financing various election campaigns. According to some reports, Korzhakov was a key figure in selecting and appointing Sergey Svechnikov, Boris Kuzyk and Alexander Kotelkin to the posts of chairman of the GKVTP, presidential adviser on military–technical cooperation and director of Rosvooruzheniye, respectively. With 'a little help from his friends', Korzhakov built up black funds to finance Yeltsin's re-election campaign in 1996.[67] Leaders of the Russian arms export machinery also created several private firms and banks which acted behind the back of official agencies.

As a result of these machinations, both the Russian state and arms producers lost millions, perhaps billions, of dollars. In a letter to the president of June 1996, Attorney General Yuriy Skuratov pointed out that Rosvooruzheniye owed $200 million to the Russian defence complex.[68] According to the state tax service, in 1997 it owed $80 million to just one defence plant—the tank producer Uralvagonzavod.[69]

[66] Sokolov, S. and Pluzhnikov, S., 'Kak torguyut oruzhiem v Rossii' [How Russia sells arms], *Novaya Gazeta*, 14 July 1997, p. 2.

[67] Sokolov and Pluzhnikov (note 66), pp. 1–3; and Klenov, V., 'Obogativshiesya "tsivilizatory" pokidayut oruzheyniy bisnes' [Enriched 'civilizers' are getting out of the arms business], *Rossiyskaya Gazeta*, 14 Feb. 1998, pp. 1–2.

[68] Sokolov and Pluzhnikov (note 66), p. 3.

[69] Latynina, Y., 'Cherez tankostroiteley VChK metit v Rosvooruzheniye' [Through tankbuilders the Provisional Extraordinary Commission takes aim at Rosvooruzheniye], *Izvestiya*, 5 Aug. 1997, p. 3.

Industrialists and trading firms were not content with the idea that Rosvooruzheniye should enjoy a monopoly on foreign trade contacts. Following a government decree of 6 May 1994,[70] a number of defence enterprises and local trading companies (e.g., Aviaexport, Aviazapchast and Promexport in Moscow, Russkoye Oruzhie in Tula and the Volga Innovation Company in Nizhniy Novgorod) were given licences for arms export operations. The defence enterprises were offered better financial conditions and services than Rosvooruzheniye was, especially with regard to the size of commissions. However, they met with a hostile reaction from Rosvooruzheniye, which accused them of incompetence and even of damaging national security.[71] As mentioned above, by the autumn of 1995 the GKVTP had cancelled most of the export licences granted to companies other than Rosvooruzheniye. Only a limited number of defence plants had direct access to the international markets.

Industrialists hoped that with the decentralization of the arms export system in 1997 they could break Rosvooruzheniye's monopoly. This did not happen. Defence plants and trading companies were allowed more freedom in looking for potential partners and implementing agreements, but Rosvooruzheniye and Promexport retained their control over the negotiating process, signing contracts and determining the financial conditions of deals. In some cases their monopoly has become even stronger. For example, Aviazapchast (which specializes in trade in spare parts for military and civilian aircraft) lost as much as 70 per cent of its profit because the right to export spare parts was transferred solely to Promexport (which had rather limited experience in this field).[72]

Thus, through the GKVTP, the KMS, the MFERC, Rosvooruzheniye and Promexport, the government has not only retained control over arms export policies but also returned to some Soviet practices of subordinating commercial to political and strategic motives for exports, centralizing procedures and neglecting producers' interests.

The government has tried from time to time to improve the management process. For example, in late 1994 it undertook an audit and

<hr>

[70] See note 26.

[71] *Izvestiya,* 10 Oct. 1995, p. 3.

[72] Korotchenko, I., 'Rossiyskie spetseksportery ukreplyayut svoi pozitsii' [The Russian special exporters strengthen their positions], *Nezavisimoye Voyennoye Obozreniye,* 8–14 May 1998, p. 6.

investigation of Rosvooruzheniye's activities after many accusations against it. According to presidential representative Marshal Yevgeniy Shaposhnikov, who held the inquiry, violations of the law and instances of corruption were discovered.[73] Many employees were dismissed and legal proceedings began against General Viktor Samoylov, the former head of Rosvooruzheniye, and a number of his colleagues. The scandal did Rosvooruzheniye substantial damage both inside the country and abroad.

Under the 'troika' of Kotelkin, Kuzyk and Svechnikov, corruption in the arms export decision-making apparatus was even worse than before. On 17 June 1996 the Attorney General began legal proceedings against Rosvooruzheniye, which was charged with misappropriation of $400 million with the help of the commercial bank Interfininvest.[74] Boris Kuzyk and his assistants (Rustam Churyakov, Sergey Mishenko and Alexander Kotelkin) and deputy (Yevgeniy Cheburayev) were involved in this case. After the resignation of Korzhakov in late June 1996 Svechnikov was also forced to resign. Kuzyk and Kotelkin, who were backed by Alexander Lebed, then the National Security Adviser to the President, survived the purge and stayed in power for another year. With the adoption of presidential decree no. 907 and the appointment of Yevgeniy Ananyev as director of Rosvooruzheniye in August 1997, the government declared that it had adequately dealt with corruption and financial machinations in the arms export system. However, most of the managerial problems are still there.

In summary, during the post-communist period Russia succeeded in establishing a decision-making system in the field of military–technical cooperation with foreign countries. The lack of stable and clear ground rules, numerous scandals and frequent reshuffles, however, have prevented this system from functioning efficiently. This has also undermined Russia's reputation as a reliable international partner. These shifts in the Russian arms export process have affected Moscow's relations with the East Asian countries.

[73] *Ponedelnik,* no. 42 (1994), pp. 2–3.
[74] Sokolov and Pluzhnikov (note 66), pp. 2–3; and Klenov (note 67), p. 2.

4. China

I. Introduction

During the early and mid-1950s, the Soviet Union provided China with a wide array of military hardware. By the early 1960s their strategic cooperation had given way to enmity and their military cooperation ceased.[1] After a 30-year period of hostility, military contacts were resumed within the framework of a policy of rapprochement established by President Mikhail Gorbachev at the May 1989 Sino-Soviet summit meeting. The two governments opened negotiations on a series of agreements on mutual force reductions, the demarcation of disputed border areas, the resumption of military-to-military exchanges and greatly expanded economic relations.

Sales of weapons and defence technology were at the heart of this new military relationship. The first discussion on arms sales began during a June 1990 visit to Moscow by General Liu Huaqing, Vice-Chairman of the Chinese Central Military Commission.[2] This was followed by extensive and frequent dialogue between the two sides on the transfer of advanced weapon systems, despite the collapse of the Soviet Union and the domestic crisis in Russia. It was President Boris Yeltsin who concluded the most extensive military agreements with China since the 1950s: after visiting Beijing in December 1992 he promised to sell China 'the most sophisticated armaments and weapons'.[3] In May 1995 then Russian Defence Minister Pavel Grachev confirmed that arms transfers would remain an essential element of the relations between China and Russia.

In contrast with the military cooperation of the 1950s, when Russia generously shared weapons and military technology with China, current Russian policy is more heavily influenced by economic than by strategic or ideological considerations.[4] At the same time, Russia

---

[1] Hickey, D. V. and Harmel, C. C., 'United States and China's military ties with the Russian republics', *Asian Affairs,* vol. 20, no. 4 (winter 1994), p. 241.

[2] Gill, B. and Taeho Kim, *China's Arms Acquisitions from Abroad: A Quest for 'Superb and Secret Weapons'*, SIPRI Research Report no. 11 (Oxford University Press: Oxford, 1995), p. 53.

[3] *Washington Post,* 19 Dec. 1992.

[4] Trenin, D., 'Kak prikryt vostochny geostrategicheskiy "fasad" Rossii?' [How to protect the eastern geo-strategic 'façade' of Russia?], *Nezavisimoye Voyennoye Obozreniye,* no. 17 (1997), p. 4.

regards China (alongside India and Kazakhstan) as an important pillar of the Eurasian security system in the post-cold war era. China made it clear that it supported Russia in its resistance to NATO enlargement. The two countries declared that their common aim was to build a 'strategic partnership'[5] but it was not by accident that they avoided using the term 'strategic alliance': as they emphasized in their joint declaration of 24 April 1997, both states oppose military bloc politics and favour a 'multi-polar world order'.[6]

Since the resumption of their military cooperation, Russia has become China's leading arms supplier (see table 4.1). According to some sources, its contracts for arms sales to China reportedly totalled between $1 billion and nearly $2 billion in 1992[7] and reached a value of $1 billion in 1994.[8] The total cost of China's purchases of Russian weapons and equipment in 1991–94 has been estimated by other sources at $4.5–6 billion.[9]

In 1995 China received arms from Russia worth $626 million. The year 1996 began with a $2 billion contract to co-produce the Su-27 (Flanker) fighter aircraft in China. In 1996 Russia delivered arms and ammunition to China worth $728 million.[10]

Sino-Russian arms deals and defence industrial cooperation have become the focal point of China's efforts to engage Russia in a substantive military relationship and to obtain advanced military equipment and technology in order to modernize the inventory of the People's Liberation Army (PLA), enhance its air and naval capabilities, and advance its power projection in East Asia.

See the register in the appendix in this volume for transfers of major conventional weapons by Russia to China in the period 1992–98.

[5] Fanlin, L., 'Strategicheskoye partnerstvo' [Strategic partnership], *Rossiyskaya Gazeta,* 22 Apr. 1997, p. 7.

[6] For the text of the declaration, see *Rossiyskaya Gazeta,* 25 Apr. 1997, p. 3.

[7] Sismanidis, R., 'China and the post-Soviet security structure', *Asian Affairs: An American Review,* vol. 21, no. 1 (spring 1994), p. 51.

[8] *Izvestiya,* 22 Sep. 1994.

[9] *Jane's Defence Weekly,* 19 Nov. 1994, reported that Russian arms sales to China in 1992–93 were worth $3–5 billion. This estimate did not include the cost of 4 Kilo Class submarines worth $1–1.5 billion. See also Skosyrev, V. 'China may delight Russian defense sector and really upset Washington', *Izvestiya,* 12 Aug. 1994, p. 3, in 'China said to spend $5 billion on Russian arms', Foreign Broadcast Information Service, *Daily Report–Central Eurasia (FBIS-SOV),* FBIS-SOV-94-157, 15 Aug. 1994, pp. 10–11; and Gill and Kim (note 2), p. 55.

[10] Platkovsky, A., 'Oruzheyny biznes na grani myasnoy voiny' [Arms business on the brink of a pork war], *Izvestiya,* 15 Mar. 1997.

Table 4.1. Value of the transfers of major conventional weapons to China by the leading suppliers, 1990–97

Figures are SIPRI trend-indicator values, expressed in US $m. at constant (1990) prices.

Supplier	1990	1991	1992	1993	1994	1995	1996	1997	Total
USSR/Russia	86	125	1 092	978	–	352	960	1 749	**5 342**
Israel	56	56	57	57	57	56	57	57	**453**
Ukraine	–	16	16	56	20	–	52	–	**160**
France	25	24	11	3	26	17	33	10	**149**
Italy	10	8	–	–	–	–	–	–	**18**
Total	**177**	**229**	**1 176**	**1 096**	**103**	**425**	**1 102**	**1 816**	**6 124**

Sources: SIPRI arms transfers database.

II. Land forces

China is estimated to have 10 000 tanks in its inventory, mostly Chinese versions of Soviet-designed main battle tanks (MBTs)[11] and most of them developed from the T-54/55 series designed in the early 1950s and now outdated. Many of its tanks are believed to be non-operational. The need to modernize the tank fleet became obvious by the end of the 1980s.

According to Russian military sources, in 1992 China agreed to buy roughly 50 T-72 MBTs and 70 BMP armoured infantry fighting vehicles (AIFVs) at a cost of about $250 million.[12] According to other unconfirmed reports, these tanks were delivered at the end of 1993.[13] The transfer involved the latest model of the heavily armed and relatively modern T-72 family—an improved version of the T-72M1. If the T-72 were to replace the immense Chinese inventory of older tanks, this would represent a major increase in China's capability.[14]

During a visit to China by President Yeltsin in April 1996 purchases of, for example, tanks, tank fire-control systems and BTR-80 armoured personnel carriers (APCs) were discussed.[15] Unconfirmed

[11] *World Defence Almanac 1993–94: The Balance of Military Power,* vol. 18, issue 1 (1994) of *Military Technology,* p. 222.

[12] *Far Eastern Economic Review*, 8 July 1993, p. 26; and *Washington Post*, 31 Mar. 1993.

[13] *Izvestiya,* 30 Mar. 1994, p. 4.

[14] Bain, W., 'Sino-Indian military modernization: the potential for destabilization', *Asian Affairs: An American Review*, vol. 21, no. 3 (fall 1994), pp. 133–34.

[15] *Jane's Defence Weekly,* 24 Apr. 1996, p. 10.

reports have suggested that China will order about 200 BMP-3s from Russia.[16]

In October 1992 the PLA became the first export customer to receive the Russian S-300PMU-1 surface-to-air missile (SAM), designated the SA-10C Grumble by NATO.[17] China has bought launchers and approximately 60 missiles for testing purposes and, according to other sources, ordered between four and six launchers with 100 missiles.[18] The PLA has no system with similar performance, and the S-300PMU-1 would give a significant boost to its air defence capabilities. The S-300PMU is a local-area, medium-range, mobile air defence system similar in mission to the US Patriot and designed originally to threaten low-flying strike aircraft.[19] Later versions (NATO designation the SA-12 Gladiator) have also been modified to protect against missile attack.[20] In this version the S-300PMU has a range of up to 100 km and a limited capability to intercept long-range ballistic missiles, precision-guided munitions and cruise missiles.[21]

Some Russian sources suggest that China in 1995 received an indefinite number of the Antey Tor-M1 (NATO designation SA-15 Gauntlet) self-propelled SAM system. It also ordered T-80U tanks and is discussing acquiring T-90C tanks and the 2S6M Tunguska combined gun/SAM system.[22] However, Russian experts deny that any T-80Us have yet been transferred.

III. The air force

Up to the resumption of military cooperation with Russia, China had a fleet of 5000 obsolete combat aircraft, most of them based on old

[16] Baliev, A., 'Obshchiye interesy velikikh sosedey' [Common interests of big neighbours], *Nezavisimoye Voyennoye Obozreniye,* no. 10 (1997).

[17] Dantes, E., 'Changing air power doctrines of regional military powers', *Asian Defence Journal,* Mar. 1993, p. 43.

[18] *World Defence Almanac 1993–94* (note 11); *Izvestiya,* 5 Mar. 1993, p. 3; Makienko, K., 'Opasno li torgovat oruzhiem s Kitaem?' [Is it dangerous to sell arms to China?], *Pro et Contra,* vol. 3, no. 1 (winter 1998), p. 46; and Gill, B., 'Trade, production, and control of conventional weapons in East Asia', 1995, p. 21, Unpublished manuscript.

[19] Isby, D., *Weapons and Tactics of the Soviet Army* (Jane's: London, 1988), p. 359.

[20] Isby (note 19); and *New York Times,* 18 Oct. 1992.

[21] *New York Times,* 18 Oct. 1992; International Institute for Strategic Studies, *The Military Balance 1993–1994* (IISS: London, 1993), p. 148; and Cheung, T. M., 'Sukhois, sams, subs', *Far Eastern Economic Review,* 8 Apr. 1993, p. 23.

[22] *Jane's International Defense Review,* Sep. 1996, p. 9; Litovkin, V., 'Kitayskaya armiya krepchayet russkim oruzhiem' [The Chinese Army is getting stronger due to Russian arms], *Izvestiya,* 25 Apr. 1997, p. 3; and Makienko (note 18), p. 46.

Soviet designs such as the MiG-21 and MiG-19 fighter aircraft and the Tu-16 bomber. Chinese helicopters are also rather obsolete and include the AS-332, Bell 214, Mi-8, Z-5 and Z-9 series.[23]

The PLA Air Force (PLAAF) has made a significant investment in domestic modernization of its equipment but with limited success. In 1990 China introduced the F-8II Finback, but this aircraft is not comparable to contemporary Western or Russian aircraft.[24] The failure of the Finback programme forced the PLAAF to seek alternative aircraft, and the dramatic reduction in tension between China and Russia made Russia an obvious choice as a supplier. In 1992 China received 26 Su-27s, Russia's most advanced air-superiority fighter, including two trainer versions.[25]

The Su-27 is designed for air-to-air combat and is equipped with Russia's most advanced avionics.[26] Among other features, it has multiple-target engagement and look-down/shoot-down capabilities. It has a combat radius of approximately 1600 km, which could be extended if China is able to acquire in-flight refuelling capability—an acquisition priority. The Su-27s are currently based at Wuhu in Anhui province near China's east coast and will primarily be used as interceptors. However, if deployed in southern China (probably on Hainan Island) they could operate over the South China Sea.[27] (Taiwanese military sources suggest that China has deployed Su-27s not only in Anhui but also in Guangdong province and that both Japan and Taiwan are within the range of these aircraft,[28] but the reliability of these sources is questionable.) The Su-27 gives the PLAAF an immediate qualitative boost.

Some Russian military experts note that the capabilities of China's Su-27s should not be overestimated. Ruslan Pukhov, of the Centre of

<hr>

[23] *World Defence Almanac 1993–94* (note 11), p. 222; and International Institute for Strategic Studies, *The Military Balance 1996/97* (Oxford University Press: Oxford, 1996), p. 181.

[24] Bin Yu, 'Sino-Russian military relations', *Asian Survey,* vol. 33, no. 3 (1993), p. 305; Jencks, H., *Some Political and Military Implications of Soviet Warplane Sales to the PRC* (Sun Yat-Sen Center for Policy Studies: Kaohsiung, 1991), pp. 5–6. It is interesting to note that China is still running 6 fighter programmes at a time when most countries are having difficulty financing 1. Bermudez, J., 'China's export mission for multi-role fighter', *Jane's Defence Weekly,* 23 Apr. 1997, p. 29.

[25] *The Military Balance 1993–1994* (note 21), p. 154; and Cheung (note 21), p. 23.

[26] Taylor, J., 'Gallery of Soviet aerospace weapons', *Air Force Magazine,* Mar. 1990, p. 75.

[27] Fulghum, D. and Proctor, P., 'Chinese coveting offensive triad', *Aviation Week & Space Technology,* 21 Sep. 1992, p. 21.

[28] *Nizhegorodskiye Novosti,* 16 Nov. 1996, p. 2.

Political Studies in Moscow, reported that the aircraft supplied to China and those that it is planning to build under licence are of the basic model rather than variants such as the Su-30MK or Su-35. The reason is the substantially lower price of the earlier version.[29] According to Major-General Sergey Karaoglanov, former chairman of Oboronexport (the predecessor of Rosvooruzheniye), only about one-third of the $1 billion Su-27 deal was payable in hard currency and the rest in consumer goods.[30]

Procurement of a further batch of 24 Su-27s (plus two twin-seater trainers) was reported in early 1995. Deliveries were expected to begin in 1995 and end 6–12 months after the first delivery. Some sources suggest that half the (undisclosed) purchase price is to be paid in hard currency and half by barter; others report that the split is more likely to be 70 : 30 in favour of hard currency.[31] An agreement in principle to begin producing the aircraft under licence was reportedly reached as well.

Some Su-27 aircraft from the second batch arrived in China to coincide with President Yeltsin's visit to China in April 1996, when he agreed that Russia would transfer a third batch. China expected to receive 72 Su-27s (plus 6 trainers) by the end of 1997.[32] The third batch is almost certainly linked directly to the licensing agreement, perhaps serving as a further inducement to Russia to transfer the required technology. It may also reflect more immediate Chinese operational requirements, as the locally built aircraft will not be available for several years. The initial production rate is likely to be limited to just 10–20 platforms annually.[33]

The Deputy Commander of the Russian Air Force Front Aviation Unit, Major-General Vladislav Davydov, suggested that 20 Chinese pilots were stationed at Krasnodar Air Base in Russia in mid-1996. He also reported that Russian pilots flew eight Su-27 single-seater fighters and three two-seater trainers to China's Suiqiu airport in July 1996. These were reportedly equipped with the Inertial Navigation System/Global Positioning System (INS/GPS) at China's request.[34] According to Army General Pyotr Deynekin, then Commander of the

[29] *Jane's International Defense Review*, Sep. 1996, p. 9.
[30] *Far Eastern Economic Review,* 3 Sep. 1992, p. 21.
[31] *Jane's Defence Weekly,* 6 May 1995, p. 3.
[32] Mufson, S., 'Muscle flexing in Pacific', *International Herald Tribune,* 12 June 1997, p. 5.
[33] *Jane's Defence Weekly,* 24 Apr. 1996, p. 10.
[34] *Jane's International Defense Review*, Sep. 1996, p. 9.

Russian Air Force, China was satisfied with the quality of its Su-27s.[35] There were also reports in the Russian press that China was to order up to 55 more Su-27s or Su-30MKs.[36]

The Su-27 deal was followed in 1992 by a contract for 100 Klimov RD-33 aircraft engines, which Russia uses to power its MiG-29 fighter and China intended to employ to upgrade its export-oriented Super F-7 fighter or—after its cancellation—the FC-1 fighter and some other aircraft.[37]

There were also reports that China was prepared to buy 24–36 MiG-31 interceptor and 40 MiG-29 fighter aircraft as well as 12 Su-24 fighter-bombers[38] but these plans were later cancelled. According to some accounts, in July 1994 China's State Council approved an additional $5 billion worth of arms imports from Russia, including an unspecified number of Su-30MK and Su-35 fighters.[39] Russia apparently refused to sell the advanced Su-35 but offered the Su-27 and the Su-30MK as an alternative.[40]

In addition to these fighter aircraft, Russia has apparently offered the supersonic Tu-22M Backfire bomber (4000-km unrefuelled range) to replace China's obsolete H-6 bomber force.[41] Although spare parts may become a problem, China's mere possession of this system, let alone any production capability, will worry its neighbours. Following President Yeltsin's April 1996 visit, China reportedly ordered 118 sets of missile systems and four Tu-22M long-range bombers.[42] These reports, however, have not been confirmed.

[35] *Jane's International Defense Review*, Sep. 1996, p. 9.

[36] *Nizhegoroskiye Novosti*, 31 Jan. 1997, p. 2; and *Jane's Defence Weekly*, 15 Jan. 1997, p. 5.

[37] Gill (note 18); and *Jane's Defence Weekly*, 22 Jan. 1994, p. 3, and 19 Feb. 1994, p. 26.

[38] Dantes (note 17), p. 43; Anthony, I. *et al.*, 'Arms production and arms trade', *SIPRI Yearbook 1993: World Armaments and Disarmament* (Oxford University Press: Oxford, 1993), p. 501; *The Military Balance 1993–1994* (note 21), p. 148; Bin Yu (note 24), pp. 308–10; *Asian Security 1994/95* (Brassey's: London, 1994), p. 15; and *Military and Arms Transfers News*, 17 June 1994, p. 5.

[39] *Asian Recorder*, 27 Aug.–2 Sep. 1994, p. 24192.

[40] *Military and Arms Transfers News*, 26 Aug. 1994, p. 5.

[41] Bain (note 14), p. 135; Blank, S. J., *Challenging the New World Order: The Arms Transfers Policies of the Russian Republic* (Strategic Studies Institute, US Army War College: Carlisle Barracks, Pa., 1993), pp. 53–60; Blank, S., 'Russia arms exports and Asia', *Asian Defence Journal*, Mar. 1994, p. 78; and Davis, M., 'Russia's big arms sales drive', *Asia–Pacific Defence Reporter*, Aug.–Sep. 1994, p. 12.

[42] 'The Sino-Russian arms bazaar', *Jane's Intelligence Review*, July 1996, p. 330. The type of missiles ordered is not specified but it is clear from the context that air-to-air or air-to-surface missiles are meant.

The Shenyang Aircraft Company concluded a deal with the Russian company Phazotron to purchase 150–200 Zhuk multi-mode radars (called the Zhuk-8 II by the company) for installation in the J-8 IIM and possibly the J-8 II fighters. The Zhuk-8 II is a pulse-Doppler radar with a 70-km search range and a tracking range of about 50 km (apparently based on the N-019 used in the MiG-29). It can operate in two modes, air-to-air and air-to-ground. In the air-to-air mode it has look-up, look-down and multiple-target tracking capabilities. It can track 10 targets and attack two of them simultaneously. In the air-to-ground mode it has mapping and ranging capabilities.[43]

In October 1990 the first significant Chinese post-détente military purchase was made from the then Soviet Union—24 Mi-17 HIP-H transport helicopters.[44] The PLAAF has taken delivery of at least 10 Ilyushin Il-76 heavy transport aircraft (the militarized version of the Il-76M), together with facilities to service them.[45] It should prove a particularly important addition, since until recently the PLAAF transport fleet had only had light and medium-size cargo aircraft. A further seven Il-76s are said to be on order.[46] They may be supplemented in the inventory by an additional 15 Il-76Ms from Uzbekistan.

There were some reports that China had also agreed to buy an unspecified number of A-50 airborne warning and control (AWAC) aircraft and long-range early-warning radar systems.[47] According to sources in China and Russia, China has finalized arrangements to acquire an airborne early-warning (AEW) capability. The AEW programme involves four main suppliers, including Russia. Ilyushin Il-76 four-turbofan long-range transports are to be obtained from Turkmenistan and refurbished in Russia, while IAI Elta Electronics in Israel is the principal contractor for system installation and some British components are reportedly included in the package. The first Il-76 is expected to arrive in Israel for refitting in 1997 and the programme is said to involve eight aircraft.[48]

China may also procure the Russian AS-15 air-launched cruise missile, which has a 3000-km range and is capable of being launched

[43] Bermudez (note 24), p. 29.
[44] Jencks (note 24), p. 15.
[45] International Institute for Strategic Studies (note 23), p. 181.
[46] *World Defence Almanac 1993–94* (note 11), p. 222.
[47] *Far Eastern Economic Review,* 8 July 1993, p. 26; and *Washington Post,* 31 Mar. 1993.
[48] *Jane's Defence Weekly,* 4 June 1997, p. 12.

by the PLAAF's B-6D bomber.[49] The status of this potential transaction remains uncertain.

If all these programmes are completed, the addition of sophisticated Russian equipment such as that discussed above will represent a spectacular improvement over current PLAAF hardware. Aircraft such as the Su-27 and the Tu-22M will give China a credible tool for military intervention beyond its borders. In lieu of actual combat, such aircraft would stand as a symbol of Chinese power and prestige and offer an effective deterrent. Modern military aircraft will also add to the PLAAF efforts to develop an effective combined-arms capability.[50]

IV. The navy

Russia has also contributed to the development of the PLA Navy (PLAN). The PLAN has 7 ex-Soviet and Chinese Romeo Class submarines (probably no longer operational), 3 Russian Kilo Class submarines (of their 1 strategic and 62 tactical submarines), 20 ex-Soviet Kronstadt Class patrol craft (of 450 vessels of this class) and 35 Soviet T-43 Class ocean minesweepers (of 121 minesweepers).[51] However, to date the PLAN has no ex-Soviet or Russian principal surface combatants (not counting two Sovremenny Class destroyers ordered by China in 1996 but not reported to have been delivered).

China has been rapidly strengthening its military preparedness, primarily because of the recently heightened concern over perceived pro-independence tendencies in Taiwan. The PLAN's lack of suitable long-range offensive capabilities was highlighted when the USA deployed two aircraft-carrier battle groups close to the Taiwan Strait in the spring of 1996. The dispute over the Spratly Islands and the

[49] Allen, K., Krumel, G. and Pollack, J. D., *China's Air Force Enters the 21st Century* (RAND: Santa Monica, Calif., 1995), p. 159.

[50] Bellows, M. (ed.), *Asia in the 21st Century: Evolving Strategic Priorities* (National Defense University Press: Washington, DC, 1994), p. 95; Sismanidis (note 7), p. 51; Hickey and Harmel (note 1), pp. 241–53; Bain (note 14), pp. 131–47; Afanasiev, E., 'Russia–China relations: from normalization to partnership', *Far Eastern Affairs* (Moscow), no. 1 (1994), pp. 3–8; Taylor, R. I. D., 'Chinese policy towards the Asia–Pacific region: contemporary perspectives', *Asian Affairs: Journal of the Royal Society for Asian Affairs*, vol. 25, pt. iii (Oct. 1994), pp. 259–69; Shambaugh, D., 'The insecurity of security: the PLA's evolving doctrine and threat perceptions towards 2000', *Journal of Northeast Asian Studies,* vol. 13, no. 1 (spring 1994), pp. 3–25; and Munro, R., 'China's waxing spheres of influence', *Orbis,* vol. 38, no. 4 (fall 1994), pp. 585–605.

[51] *World Defence Almanac 1993–94* (note 11), p. 221; and *The Military Balance 1996/97* (note 23), p. 180.

growth of Japanese sea power have also given China an immediate incentive to modernize its naval forces.

China is said to attach high priority to modernizing its navy along with the air force.[52] Naval modernization includes the introduction of a new class of destroyer, new conventionally and nuclear-powered submarines, and substantial talk of acquiring an aircraft-carrier. According to some assessments, this programme suggests that China aims to move from a brown-water coastal navy to one that is capable of projecting power into the Pacific and Indian oceans.[53]

Sino-Russian military–technical cooperation in the naval field started in 1991. In February 1994 the Nizhniy Novgorod Mashzavod plant signed a contract with the PLAN to supply three ship-borne 77-mm automatic artillery systems. In March 1995 Chinese specialists were trained at Mashzavod to use these guns, which were to be delivered by the end of the year.[54]

The PLAN is also modernizing its submarine fleet. In 1994 China bought four Kilo Class (877.EKM) submarines from Russia and apparently intends to obtain the rights to manufacture additional vessels in China.[55] The first was delivered as early as February 1995[56] and the second and third in 1996–97.[57] The fourth was expected to be delivered by the end of 1998.[58] The first and second vessels were produced at the Krasnoye Sormovo plant (Nizhniy Novgorod), the third and fourth at the Admiralteyskie Shipyard (St Petersburg). The fourth submarine is the last one produced under the 877.EKM project in Russia.[59] Some reports contend that China may ultimately obtain up to 22 Kilo submarines, but sources in China with a closer knowledge of the programme dismiss this.[60] It was reported in March 1995 that China had struck another deal with Russia for the purchase of six

[52] Glaser, B., 'China's security perceptions: interests and ambitions', *Asian Survey*, vol. 33, no. 3 (1993), p. 265.

[53] Bain (note 14), p. 136.

[54] *Birzha*, 14 Apr. 1994, p. 3.

[55] Cheung (note 21), p. 23; Cheung, T. M., 'China's buying spree', *Far Eastern Economic Review*, 8 July 1993, p. 26; and Bain (note 14), p. 137.

[56] *Delo*, 7–13 Apr. 1995, p. 3.

[57] Markov, D., 'More details surface of Rubin's Kilo plans', *Jane's Intelligence Review*, May 1997, p. 215.

[58] Putilov, S., 'Proshalnaya gastrol Varshavyanki' [The final tour of Varshavyanka], *Nezavisimoye Voyennoye Obozreniye*, 20–26 Mar. 1998, p. 8.

[59] Putilov (note 58), p. 8.

[60] *Jane's Defence Weekly*, 13 May 1995, p. 18.

more submarines,[61] but only the order of two Type 636 submarines is confirmed.[62]

The Kilo is considered to be an advanced conventionally powered vessel that is extremely effective in the coastal defence role. With a range of 9650 km and an ability to remain at sea for up to 45 days,[63] these vessels represent a significant addition not only to the PLA's coastal defence but also to its offensive potential. The PLAN has also become the first export customer for the Type 636 variant of the Kilo.[64] The Type 636 is a slightly larger and quieter derivative, featuring improved sonar and a longer range.[65]

There have been numerous reports that China may buy several Sovremenny Class destroyers from Russia. These ships have formidable air defence and anti-ship capabilities and can accommodate anti-submarine warfare (ASW) helicopters.[66] Russia has persistently denied that Sovremennys were on offer.[67] China first asked Russia to sell it two Sovremennys in 1994, after difficult negotiations, especially over the price and terms of payment. Since China and Russia reportedly agreed in November 1996 that all future arms transfers would be fully paid for in hard currency, this facilitated the signing of the contract. Growing urgency on the part of the PLAN to expand its operational capabilities may also have helped accelerate agreement on the destroyer deal.

A deal for two Sovremenny destroyers worth $800 million was finalized during a visit to Moscow by Chinese Premier Li Peng in late December 1996,[68] although no mention of the agreement was made in the official communiqué issued at the conclusion of the visit. The destroyers will come from St Petersburg's North Yard, but it is unclear whether they will be purpose-built or whether China will gain quicker delivery by accepting the last two ships of the class under construction for the Russian Navy. Completion of these and the first of an improved Sovremenny II Class has been delayed because of

[61] *Asian Recorder,* 26 Mar.–1 Apr. 1995, p. 24672; and *Jane's Defence Weekly,* 18 Mar. 1995, p. 3.

[62] Putilov (note 58), p. 8.

[63] On the 877.EKM and Type 636 Kilo projects, see Markov (note 57), p. 211.

[64] Scott, R., 'Kilo sale adds to Russia's exports', *Pointer,* Oct. 1996, p. 1; and Markov (note 57), pp. 211, 215.

[65] Markov (note 57), pp. 209–11.

[66] Preston, A., 'Russian weapons and ships in the Asia–Pacific region', *Asian Defence Journal,* Dec. 1992, p. 60.

[67] *Jane's International Defense Review,* Sep. 1996, p. 9.

[68] *Jane's Defence Weekly,* 15 Jan. 1997, p. 5.

funding shortages. It could take two or three years to modify and fully fit the vessels currently under construction, analysts say.[69]

The Sovremenny Class, which first entered Soviet service in 1980, is primarily a surface strike combatant. Ships are normally armed with eight launchers for the sea-skimming SS-N-22 Sunburn surface-to-surface missile (SSM), which has a range of up to 150 km, two SA-N-17 Grizzly SAM launchers and two twin 130-mm guns. The Chinese vessels are likely to be an improved version of the original design with provision for up to 24 Sunburn SSMs.[70]

The 7000-tonne warship is much bigger, more sophisticated and much more heavily armed than the 4200-tonne Luhu Class destroyer, China's latest and largest surface combatant. China has two Luhus but further production has been suspended because of difficulties in obtaining additional General Electric LM-2500 gas turbine engines, which are subject to the US sanctions imposed after the Tiananmen Square incident in 1989. The two destroyers will substantially enhance the PLAN's surface strike capabilities and its ability to deploy over long distances.

According to Tai Ming Cheung, the clearest sign of China's blue-water aspirations is its aircraft-carrier plans.[71] Since the late 1980s, China has been examining an off-the-shelf purchase of an aircraft-carrier hull and has sent teams to inspect French, Indian, Italian, Russian, Spanish and Ukrainian carriers. There have been frequent reports that China was interested in the Ukrainian ship *Varyag*—a large unfinished carrier that was part of the disputed Soviet Black Sea Fleet—in acquiring a smaller Russian carrier or in building a 30 000- to 48 000-tonne vessel domestically.[72] Other reports suggest that China might buy the French carrier *Clemenceau*. This could be the priority for China because it intends to use a potential deal to persuade

---

[69] *Jane's Defence Weekly,* 15 Jan. 1997, p. 5.

[70] *Jane's Defence Weekly,* 15 Jan. 1997, p. 5.

[71] Cheung, T. M., *Growth of Chinese Naval Power* (Institute of Southeast Asian Studies: Singapore, 1990), p. 27. See also *New York Times,* 11 Jan. 1993; Ball, D., 'A new era in confidence building: the second-track process in the Asia/Pacific region', *Security Dialogue,* vol. 25, no. 2 (June 1994), pp. 159–60; and Lin, C., 'Chinese military modernization: perceptions, progress and prospects', *Security Studies,* vol. 3, no. 4 (summer 1994), p. 731.

[72] *New York Times,* 11 Jan. 1993; Cheung (note 71); and Ryan, S., 'The PLA Navy's search for a blue water capability', *Asian Defence Journal,* no. 5 (1994), p. 30. With the Sovremenny Class destroyer and Kilo Class submarine programmes costing over $2 billion, some analysts contend this means there is little likelihood that the PLAN can find sufficient funds for an aircraft-carrier before the turn of the century. *Jane's Defence Weekly,* 15 Jan. 1997, p. 5.

the West to lift the arms embargo imposed after the 1989 Tiananmen Square incident; the *Clemenceau*'s impressive capability or price may be secondary considerations.[73]

In March 1998 the Ukrainian Government decided to sell the *Varyag* to a tourism firm registered in Macau for $20 million for use as a floating hotel. However, the local authorities did not permit the firm to moor the vessel in Macau harbour. It also emerged that the firm has no licence, no real address and assets of only $125 000, so it is unclear how it could afford the deal. Many Russian experts believe that the *Varyag* has been bought by the PLAN to be completed locally or used for copying the technology.[74]

Although there is no confirmation of China's intentions to acquire an aircraft-carrier, initial training of naval officers began almost a decade ago and a dummy deck was constructed at Beijing North military airfield for deck landing and deck handling trials with the J-8-III naval fighter.[75] Another indication of a genuine interest in an aircraft-carrier was the attention paid to the Yak-141 vertical and short take-off and landing (V/STOL) naval fighter aircraft (this development programme has since been cancelled). Bin Yu argues that it is no coincidence that China purchased the Su-27 for the PLAAF since it can be modified for use on board an aircraft-carrier.[76] Numerous sources have suggested that, after the completion of the existing Su-27 deal, a follow-on purchase may include the Su-27K, the naval variant specially designated for carrier operations.[77] According to other accounts, other Russian equipment, including the Su-25 strike aircraft and MiG-29K naval fighter, could be sought. MiG-MAPO has recently begun demonstrating the MiG-29 naval version to China and India, indicating perhaps that the larger, more complex naval version of the Su-27 is not the sole maritime fighter on offer.[78] Eventual deployment of any aircraft by the air force in a maritime strike role would further boost the PLAN's offensive capabilities.

[73] *Le Monde,* 11 Oct. 1996, p. 4. See also Lewis, J. A. C., 'France ready to resume arms trade with China', *Jane's Defence Weekly,* 16 Apr. 1997, p. 3; and Beaver, P., 'China looks to Europe for carrier', *Jane's Intelligence Review and Jane's Sentinel Pointer,* Dec. 1996, p. 1.

[74] *Rossiyskaya Gazeta,* 21 Mar. 1998, p. 1; and Batygin, A., 'Komu prodayetsya posledniy Varyag?' [To whom is the last Varyag selling?], *Rossiyskaya Gazeta,* 27 Mar. 1998, p. 23.

[75] Beaver (note 73), p. 1.

[76] Bin Yu (note 24), pp. 302, 308.

[77] Dantes (note 17), p. 43; Ackerman, J. and Dunn, M., 'Chinese airpower revs up', *Air Force Magazine,* July 1993, p. 59; and *Military and Arms Transfers News,* 7 Oct. 1994, p. 4.

[78] Beaver (note 73), p. 1.

Moreover, if the PLAN were also to purchase the naval variant of the S-300PMU (NATO designation SA-N-6), it would possess the foundation for building an adequate defensive and escort force for an aircraft-carrier.[79] In summary, there are grounds to believe that China is serious about acquiring an aircraft-carrier, but it remains unclear whether import or domestic production will be preferred.

Although Chinese officials can cogently argue that the Taiwan problem and the Spratly Islands dispute demand that China modernize its naval capabilities, these disputes are not the underlying or fundamental reasons for Chinese aspirations for a blue-water navy. Weapon platforms such as the Xia Class SSBN (nuclear-powered, ballistic-missile submarine) have little military value in such disputes. Furthermore, the cost of an aircraft-carrier and its associated escort vessels and air wing make it prohibitively expensive for use against the ASEAN countries, with their rather weak navies. Chinese military interests in the Spratlys would probably be better served by warships covered by long-range and aerial-refuelled aircraft from the Paracel Islands. An aircraft-carrier, as well as China's nuclear-powered submarines, would be much better suited for use on the open seas than in the relatively shallow and constricted waters of the South China Sea.[80]

V. Military technology transfer

Chinese military technology is as much as 20 years behind that of the West. Past efforts to resolve this problem through reverse engineering (often of Soviet military technology) have not closed this gap. China's military industry has a well-documented history of problems with reverse-engineered systems and some Chinese copies of foreign-designed weapons, such as the Soviet T-62 tank and MiG-23 fighter-bomber, have never reached the production stage.

Since resuming military cooperation with Russia, China has been extremely cautious in signing deals to purchase Russian military hardware. Chinese officials would prefer to purchase technology and production licences rather buy equipment 'off the shelf'. Some reports suggest that China would like to shift the ratio of purchases of weapons and technology, which is currently 70 : 30 in favour of the

[79] Hickey and Harmel (note 1), p. 242. The source does not mention the type of platform on which this system could be mounted.

[80] Bain (note 14), p. 137.

latter.[81] This is probably partly because of budget restrictions and partly because of fear of the potential political consequences of over-dependence on any one supplier. China would prefer to modernize its defence industry. In its pursuit of defence industrial cooperation, it has found Russia a more willing partner than Western countries. Russia has been prepared to consider transfers of advanced technology even at the risk of a long-term adverse impact on the regional balance of power. This willingness has stemmed from the desperate economic straits of the Russian defence industry and pressure from the defence industry and defence ministry officials to overrule the objections of their foreign ministry counterparts.

The military–industrial complexes of the two countries are developing about 100 joint projects. Of these, about 30 are targeted at adapting Russian basic models to Chinese standards; the remainder should result in the creation of new weapon systems and ammunition.[82]

As mentioned above, in 1995 Russia agreed to produce the Su-27 aircraft in China. The deal, revealed in Moscow in February 1996, is worth $2 billion at a conservative estimate and will probably take the form of a complex cash and barter arrangement. The licensed production deal was covered by a letter of intent that should be finalized once the second batch of Su-27s is delivered and paid for. A two-stage programme was proposed, the first being assembly in China from kits produced in Russia and the second full production in China (probably at the Shenyang Aircraft Factory). The eventual aim is thought to be production of 90–100 aircraft annually, but observers say it will probably be half that number, beginning at a rate of 10–20 aircraft per year.[83]

The variant to be produced in China is uncertain, although analysts predict it will be the improved Su-27SMK with greater multi-role capability. China would be the first customer for the type. The SMK adds extra hardpoints for stores and carries additional fuel.[84] Its precision navigation avionics, the emphasis on air-to-surface 'smart' weaponry and the ability to carry the new AA-12 active air-to-air

---

[81] Litovkin (note 22).
[82] Baliev (note 16).
[83] *Jane's Defence Weekly,* 6 May 1995, p. 3.
[84] *Jane's Defence Weekly,* 14 Feb. 1996, p. 12.

missile (AAM) would bring a significant advance in China's ability to mount both offensive maritime strike and counter-strike missions.[85]

Some Russian sources suggest that the Su-27 licence does not cover co-production of engines. If this is true, the French SNECMA company can probably provide China with a licence. In September 1996 SNECMA received the French Government's permission to study the Chinese market,[86] but the prospects for this project remain uncertain.

Sukhoi bureau officials also reportedly proposed co-production of the Su-35 in China on the condition that China buy close to 120 of the aircraft produced.[87]

It has been suggested that China is negotiating with Russian officials for a technology exchange that could include joint development of an advanced fighter aircraft 'with capabilities falling midway between the MiG-29 fighter and the MiG-31 high-altitude interceptor'.[88] According to other accounts, Russia will move some production of the MiG-31 to China. It has been suggested that 150–300 MiG-31 Foxhounds could be made in China over an eight-year period.[89] This is a high-altitude interceptor with superior extended-range radar and multiple-target engagement capabilities.[90] However, in view of the Su-27 co-production programme and China's budget constraints, these plans seem unlikely.

Another report suggests that Russia offered to develop a completely new fighter for the PLAAF for as little as $500 million. Senior Russian MOD officials have said that there have been negotiations over a deal which could result in Russian aerospace firms providing up to two-thirds of the required technical and design work, as well as the avionics and an engine, for a new fighter based on the Xinjian J-10 airframe. China is supposedly planning to produce the new aircraft at the rate of 100 per year, according to Russian statements.[91] The Chengdu-built aircraft, due to fly in 1996, should be fitted with the

[85] 'China secures deal to build "Flanker" fighters', *Jane's Defence Weekly,* 14 Feb. 1996, p. 12.

[86] Kovalenko, Y., 'V Kitaye Moskva stolknyetsya s interesami Frantsii' [Moscow will confront French interests in China], *Izvestiya,* 7 May 1997.

[87] Taeho Kim, *The Dynamics of Sino-Russian Military Relations: An Asian Perspective* (Chinese Council of Advanced Policy Studies: Taipei, 1994), p. 19.

[88] Cheung, 'China's buying spree' (note 56), p. 24.

[89] Dantes (note 17), p. 43; *World Defence Almanac 1993–94* (note 11), p. 222; *The Military Balance 1993–1994* (note 21), p. 148; and Bin Yu (note 24), pp. 308–10.

[90] Taylor (note 26), p. 75.

[91] Gallaher, M., 'China's illusory threat to the South China Sea', *International Security,* vol. 19, no. 1 (summer 1994), p. 175; and *Jane's Defence Weekly,* 19 Feb. 1994, p. 28.

Russian radar system and engines of the Su-27. The first flight test of the Phazotron radar system on board the F-10 was scheduled for 1997, according to Russian industry officials. However, no information on such tests is available. The radar is similar to the Zhuk system being installed in the F-8II M fighter upgrade programme in China. A Russian radar system may have been preferred because of China's insistence on licensed production in China.[92]

The single-engined F-10 is believed to be in the same performance and weight class as the Eurofighter 2000 and Dassault Rafale. One analyst has suggested that, if pursued, such a programme would provide China with its 'first step towards a new manufacturing capability' that could both replenish and modernize the air force's obsolete fleet of aircraft, as well as compete with Western manufacturing in the lucrative Asian arms market.[93] However, considering China's previous experience in developing modern fighter aircraft, it is safe to predict that this programme will be difficult and lengthy, even with Russian assistance. There are also some doubts that China will be able to produce anything comparable to these European aircraft.

Other assessments suggest that Chinese efforts to draw on the military technology of the former Soviet Union may not help the PLA very much in its drive to upgrade its combat power. The Russian military R&D apparatus will take many years to rebuild. Unless China can learn to develop and produce modern military equipment itself, the PLA faces a high probability of remaining locked into technological obsolescence.[94]

China is also planning to upgrade 200–300 of its F-7 fighter aircraft with new radar and avionics. The likely contenders for this programme are FIAR (Italy), Elta (Israel) and Phazotron (Russia). China is believed to be more interested in production capability, which could favour the Russian offer of the Kopyo-derived Super Komar radar.[95]

In addition to advanced fighter technology, China has been trying to acquire in-flight refuelling capabilities from Russia, which could enable the PLAAF to extend its reach. China is developing its next-generation fighter (the F-10) and such technology transfers at rela-

[92] *Jane's Defence Weekly,* 25 Nov. 1995, p. 4.

[93] Mecham, M., 'China updates its military, but business comes first', *Aviation Week & Space Technology,* 15 Mar. 1993, p. 58.

[94] Gallaher (note 91), pp. 180–81.

[95] Bickers, C., 'Russia, Israel helping China build new fighter', *Jane's Defence Weekly,* 25 Nov. 1995, p. 4.

tively concessional prices would be of considerable help. China is also attempting to purchase ASW technology and technical data on the design and construction of airframes.

China has shown keen interest in acquiring missile technologies from systems known to be capable of being equipped with multiple independently-targetable re-entry vehicles (MIRVs). According to a leaked US Defense Intelligence Agency (DIA) report, China has been attempting to acquire SS-18 (Russian designation RS-20) Satan intercontinental ballistic missile (ICBM) technology, possibly including engine and guidance technology, from Russia and/or Ukraine. China has made no secret of this, claiming that it would be used to improve its commercial space launch capabilities. The SS-18 Satan is a 'fourth-generation', two-stage, liquid-fuel missile which can deliver either a single warhead or up to 10 re-entry vehicles. According to the DIA, the PLA's interest in the SS-18 is probably linked to China's strategic force modernization.[96] Some experts suggest that with Russia's assistance China will be able to produce an ICBM with a range of up to 12 000 km (instead of the current 8000 km) by 2005.[97] With such a missile China could threaten not only the Asia–Pacific region but also the United States and Europe.

In May 1996 US Defense Secretary William Perry confirmed that China had been seeking to obtain SS-18 technology from Russia and possibly Ukraine. 'We believe that it would be a significant mistake to transfer the SS-18 technology to China and have so represented our position to the Russian Government and the Ukrainian Government', Perry said.[98] The USA would agree to allow SS-18 boosters to be used commercially as space launch vehicles, but only under tight controls, Perry indicated.

China has also reportedly received information on the SS-24 Scalpel and SS-25 Sickle ICBMs, designed at Russia's Nadiradze Design Bureau and Ukraine's Southern Machine-Building Plant. This information could prove useful since both missiles are MIRV-capable. The SS-24 (Russian designation RS-22 or RT-23U) is a rail-mobile and silo-based solid-fuel ICBM that can carry up to 10 MIRVed warheads.

[96] Lamson, J. and Bowen, W., 'One arrow, three stars: China's MIRV programme', *Jane's Intelligence Review*, June 1997, p. 267.

[97] Kovalenko (note 86).

[98] *Jane's Defence Weekly,* 29 May 1996, p. 3.

The SS-25 (Russian designation RS-12M Topol) is a road-mobile solid-fuel ICBM that can be armed with single or multiple warheads.[99]

In June 1996 *Nihon Keizai Shimbun* reported that China had purchased computer simulation technology from Russia to simulate the testing of multiple nuclear explosions and/or to design multiple-warhead missiles. However, a spokesman for Russia's Ministry of Atomic Energy (Minatom) subsequently denied this report.[100]

Military technology transfers were combined with exchanges of personnel and expertise. According to Russian MOD sources, 'more than 1000 Russian defence scientists and technicians have travelled to China since 1991 on defence-industrial exchanges [and] . . . there are around 300–400 Chinese defence specialists in Russia'.[101] It was reported that 300 of these Russian experts remained with long-term commitments.[102] Some of the Russian scientists now believed to be based permanently in China are apparently experts 'in the fields of cruise missiles, anti-submarine warfare, missile launching experiments and nuclear explosions'.[103] Chinese defence scientists and technicians are working at Russian aerospace institutes, including some in Moscow, Ryazan, Samara and Saratov. Some are studying at organizations such as the Central Institute of Aircraft Dynamics in Moscow.[104]

Some sources have suggested that Russia's chaotic economic, social and political conditions have permitted China to recruit scientists and acquire technology without official approval. For example, former US Ambassador to China James Lilley claims that 3000 Russian defence scientists and engineers were recruited by China for salaries as high as $2000 per month plus housing, a car and living expenses.[105] In late January 1996 a former employee of the Ukrainian Southern Machine Building Plant in Dnepropetrovsk, which specializes in SS-18 R&D and production, assisted three visiting Chinese representatives in ille-

---

[99] Lamson and Bowen (note 96), p. 267.

[100] Lamson and Bowen (note 96), p. 267.

[101] Cheung, 'China's buying spree' (note 56), p. 24.

[102] Hull, A. and Markov, D., 'Trends in the arms market', *Jane's Intelligence Review*, May 1997, p. 233.

[103] 'Peking recruits Russian weapons experts: report', Central News Agency (Taipei), 29 Dec. 1992; Hickey and Harmel (note 1), p. 243; *Wall Street Journal,* 14 Oct. 1993; and Shulong Chu, 'The Russian–US military balance in the post-cold war Asia–Pacific region and the "China threat"', *Journal of Northeast Asian Studies*, spring 1994, pp. 89–90.

[104] *Jane's Defence Weekly,* 19 Feb. 1994, p. 28.

[105] Hull and Markov (note 102), p. 233.

gally procuring rocket engine designs (later confiscated).[106] In mid-1992, offers were made by China 'through private channels' to nuclear scientists from the Zheleznogorsk Mining and Chemical Combine (Krasnoyarsk-26) to upgrade the uranium enrichment facility in Lanzhou.[107]

Thanks to the electronic revolution, scientists no longer have to travel abroad to assist a foreign partner. In 1993, Russian defence laboratories and their Chinese counterparts were linked by electronic mail.[108]

Many of these reports should be assessed with great caution. They clearly underestimate the Russian security services' control over defence specialists and overestimate China's ability to offer attractive financial conditions for Russian specialists, given its budget constraints. As Shulong Chu has put it, 'Reports that China recruits thousands of Russian weapons experts may come from speculation, because there is no government source from China or Russia of such [an] exchange programme. The Russian Government has lost a lot in controlling its society, but it has not lost everything'.[109]

VI. Defence industry conversion

China and Russia have agreed to strengthen their cooperation in conversion programmes. China's military industry has sharply increased its production of civilian goods: according to Chinese sources, civilian products accounted for 80 per cent of the industrial output of China's arms-producing companies in 1995.[110]

A Sino-Russian document was signed in 1994 similar to that signed the same year by China and the United States.[111] A number of joint ventures have been set up to develop conversion programmes. The companies involved in the first venture are Xing-Yui-Ju (Beijing), Yuilang Trading (Hong Kong), the Nizhniy Novgorod-based Impex and the Institute of Applied Physics at the Russian Academy of

---

[106] Lamson and Bowen (note 96), p. 267.

[107] Moody, R. A., 'Armageddon for hire', *Jane's International Defense Review*, Feb. 1997, pp. 22–23.

[108] Hull and Markov (note 102), p. 234.

[109] Shulong Chu (note 103), p. 91.

[110] *International Herald Tribune,* 10 Oct. 1996, p. 7.

[111] *Izvestiya,* 19 Oct. 1994, p. 4.

Sciences.[112] This joint venture will re-configure electro-optical defence items to create commercial laser, electro-optic and optical devices for sale in the Middle East. Russia will provide the researchers and expertise, leaving manufacturing and marketing to China.

The Sungari joint venture, set up by the Ural Device-Building Plant in Yekaterinburg and the Kharbin Commercial Trade Company, has started production of car tape recorders at the former Lazur defence plant in Nizhniy Novgorod.[113] In 1992–93 there was also a plan to convert a Russian tank repair plant near Chita on the border with China into a car factory with the help of Chinese engineers, and China was building a video recorder plant in Zelenogorsk near Moscow and modernizing a Russian tractor factory near Krasnoyarsk. Russian technicians meanwhile were renovating Soviet-built industrial plants like the Baotou steel plant, the fifth biggest in China.[114]

VII. Other programmes

In addition to arms sales, technology transfers and conversion, China and Russia have agreed to other forms of military cooperation. In 1994 their defence ministers signed an agreement to prevent incidents such as those involving the combat aircraft of one country crossing into the other's airspace. It also regulates unannounced missile launches, the use of lasers which could harm the other side and the jamming of communications equipment.[115] The agreement, which entered into force immediately and set up mechanisms for mutual security, will be reviewed annually.[116]

A September 1994 communiqué issued by Yeltsin and Chinese President Jiang Zemin mentioned confidence- and security-building measures (CSBMs), including no-first-use of nuclear weapons and the

[112] Beaver, P., 'Russian industry feels the cold', *Jane's Defence Weekly,* 7 May 1994, p. 30.

[113] *Nizhegorodskiye Novosti,* 14 Apr. 1995, p. 2.

[114] Klintworth, G., 'China and East Asia', eds R. Thakur and C. A. Thayer, *Reshaping Regional Relations: Asia–Pacific and the Former Soviet Union* (Westview Press: Boulder, Colo., 1993), p. 133.

[115] *Asian Recorder,* 6–12 Aug. 1994, p. 24144.

[116] Russia has signed similar agreements with Canada, Greece and the USA. Kyodo News Service, 12 July 1994; *NOD & Conversion,* no. 30 (Sep. 1994), p. 42; and *Military and Arms Transfers News,* 15 July 1994, p. 8.

re-targeting of nuclear missiles away from each other's territory.[117] In late 1994 agreements were signed on military cooperation, including joint naval exercises. CSBMs were initiated in 1994 between the border security forces of China and Russia.[118] By 1997 about 200 Chinese officers had been trained in Russian military academies.[119] By 1998 Russia and China had settled all the important issues regarding the demarcation of their common borders.

The two countries have significantly reduced their forces in the border areas. In 1992 Russia completed the withdrawal of troops from Mongolia initiated by Gorbachev in 1987. In May 1996 Defence Minister Grachev said that since 1995 Russia had cut 150 000 troops from deployment in the far east and that the Pacific Fleet had been reduced by 50 per cent since 1985.[120]

During President Yeltsin's April 1996 visit, China and Russia concluded an agreement on the scale and nature of military exercises in their border areas. However, while the Chinese delegation proposed moving its troops 200 km from the border, the Russians claimed that this would cause them 'technical' difficulties.[121]

On 24 April 1997 China, Kazakhstan, Kyrgyzstan, Russia and Tajikistan concluded the Treaty on Mutual Reduction of Military Forces in Border Areas, primarily intended to control troop levels within a 100-km band on either side of the borders concerned.[122] It specifies limits for the numbers of border guard troops[123] and envisages reductions in conventional land forces, tactical aviation and air defence aircraft only. It does not cover strategic forces, navies, strategic aviation or air defence missiles. If ratified by all four states, the treaty will run until 2020.

Significantly, China and Russia have resumed intelligence ties. Although details of their intelligence pact remain unknown, US officials confirm that ties were restored in September 1992.[124] The two

[117] Harada, C., *Russia and North-east Asia,* Adelphi Paper no. 310 (International Institute for Strategic Studies: London, 1997), pp. 39–40; and Menon, R., 'The strategic convergence between Russia and China', *Survival,* vol. 39, no. 2 (summer 1997), p. 108.

[118] Menon (note 117), pp. 108–109.

[119] Litovkin (note 22).

[120] Menon (note 117), p. 107.

[121] *Jane's Intelligence Review*, June 1996, p. 280.

[122] According to some accounts, quotas were established for these 4 CIS countries: 130 000 servicemen (of which 120 000 are Russian troops), 3900 tanks, 5800 APCs and AIFVs, 4500 artillery pieces, 290 aircraft and 434 helicopters. *Izvestiya,* 15 Apr. 1997, p. 3.

[123] *Rossiyskaya Gazeta,* 25 Apr. 1997, p. 3.

[124] *Washington Times,* 21 Oct. 1992.

governments will probably share information and/or opinions about mutual security concerns in the region, including the volatile situation in Central Asia and the military posture of Japan.[125]

VIII. Conclusions

The scope and results of Sino-Russian military cooperation are impressive, especially in view of the former enmity between them and the speed of their rapprochement. However, this cooperation should not be overestimated: it is far from being a relationship of real allies in terms of depth and openness. Despite the seriousness of the partners, their motives are fairly pragmatic and sometimes selfish. There is no real cordiality or frankness in their relations. They are cautious and even suspicious of each other's intentions and motives. Both are concerned with their own national interests. Russia does not permit the export of its most advanced weapon systems and technologies and is not completely satisfied with the financial conditions of its arms deals with China. China is concerned about the risk of over-dependence on Russian arms supplies and is trying to diversify its sources of armaments. It is unlikely that the two countries will abandon all their concerns and suspicions and radically change the very nature of their relationship, at least not in the foreseeable future. Regardless of their common interests, they will keep some distance between them where military and security matters are concerned.

[125] Cheung, T. M., 'Arm in arm', *Far Eastern Economic Review,* 12 Nov. 1992, p. 28.

5. South-East Asia

I. Introduction

Many Western experts believe that Russia's role in South-East Asia[1] can only be considered to be marginal at best since it is confined primarily to the diplomatic level.[2] However, the Russian foreign policy and economic elites would not agree with that assessment.

Russia has been bidding to enhance its relationship with South-East Asia in both the economic and the military areas. Russian experts believe that Moscow should keep an eye on the turbulent processes developing in the region because they may determine not only the future strategic environment in the Asia–Pacific region but also the 'face' of the 21st century.[3] As then Russian Foreign Minister Yevgeniy Primakov put it at the July 1996 meeting of the Association of South-East Asian Nations Post Ministerial Conference (ASEAN–PMC),[4] Russia is eager to build a multi-polar world in which the ASEAN 'pole' is significant.[5] ASEAN is important for Russia not only in the global sense but also in the regional context because it represents a counterbalance to any resurgent power such as China or Japan.[6] Russia also became a dialogue partner in the ASEAN Regional Forum (ARF) in 1996.[7] It suggested a broad agenda for the ARF for years to come, ranging from discussions on tensions on the Korean peninsula and the Spratly Islands to the adoption of a regional code of conduct, the development of a nuclear weapon-free zone in South-East Asia,[8] cooperation in fighting the drugs trade, space

---

[1] South-East Asia is defined here as consisting of Brunei, Cambodia, Indonesia, Laos, Malaysia, Myanmar, the Philippines, Singapore, Thailand and Viet Nam.

[2] See, e.g., Yahuda, M., *The International Politics of the Asia–Pacific, 1945–1995* (Routledge: London and New York, 1996), p. 259.

[3] Titarenko, M., 'S novymi podkhodami navstrechu 21 veku' [Facing the 21st century with new approaches], *Problemy Dalnego Vostoka*, no. 1 (1997), pp. 4–9.

[4] For the membership of ASEAN, see chapter 1, note 5, in this volume. The ASEAN–PMC is a forum for discussions of political and security issues between the ASEAN members and Australia, Canada, the European Union, Japan, South Korea, New Zealand and the USA.

[5] *Diplomaticheskiy Vestnik*, no. 8 (1996), p. 39.

[6] Abazov, R., 'Dialogue between Russia and ASEAN', *International Affairs* (Moscow), vol. 42, no. 5/6 (1996), pp. 89–90.

[7] The members of ARF are the ASEAN states plus Australia, Cambodia, Canada, China, the European Union, India, Japan, South Korea, Laos, Myanmar, New Zealand, Papua New Guinea, Russia and the USA.

[8] The Treaty on the South-East Asia Nuclear Weapon-Free Zone (Treaty of Bangkok) was opened for signature on 15 Dec. 1995 and entered into force on 27 Mar. 1997.

research and railway construction, and the development of the 'Greater Mekong' zone. Russia also organized an international seminar on security and stability in the Asia–Pacific in April 1996.[9]

ASEAN's growing prosperity, its ageing military systems, US reluctance to export some advanced weaponry and technologies to the region, the high prestige of the militaries and the fears of China combined to create powerful incentives for these countries to turn to the world arms market. According to the assessments of some Russian military experts, the countries of the region are starting military modernization programmes worth $90 billion.[10] This, as well as commercial motives, attract Russia to the ASEAN market, but the arms transfers also offer Russia the prospect of a re-entry into the strategic calculations of the regional players. As early as 1992, then Russian Foreign Minister Andrey Kozyrev told the ASEAN Annual Ministerial Meeting that Russia was 'prepared to develop cooperation in the military and military technological area with the ASEAN states with the aim of maintaining their security at the level of reasonable sufficiency'.[11] Russia has since made great strides in this direction.

The Russian approach to military cooperation with South-East Asia has varied from country to country. This chapter reviews seven of these countries with which Russian cooperation has become significant.

II. Myanmar

Since the late 1980s Myanmar (Burma) has depended on China for most of its military equipment.[12] The de-ideologization of Russian arms transfer policies and Myanmar's decision to modernize its armed forces have opened new prospects for military–technical cooperation between Myanmar and Russia.

In 1995 Myanmar ordered from Russia seven Mil Mi-17-1B twin-turbine multi-purpose helicopters; a year later it ordered five addi-

<hr>

[9] *Diplomaticheskiy Vestnik,* no. 8 (1996), pp. 35–36. See also Zhiliaev, B., 'Partnership with ASEAN', *International Affairs* (Moscow), vol. 42, no. 4 (1996), pp. 39–42.

[10] Litovkin, V., 'Dorogu indoneziyskim Su prolozhili malayziskiye Migi' [The Malaysian MiGs paved the way for the Indonesian Su aircraft], *Izvestiya,* 7 Aug. 1997, p. 3.

[11] Blank, S. J., *Challenging the New World Order: The Arms Transfers Policies of the Russian Republic* (Strategic Studies Institute, US Army War College: Carlisle Barracks, Pa., 1993), p. 61.

[12] On progress in strategic cooperation between Myanmar and China, see Rodman, P. W., 'China woos Burma', *International Herald Tribune,* 30 May 1997, p. 8.

tional Mi-17s, although neither the cost nor the delivery schedule for the second batch has been announced. The contract also included unspecified 'surface equipment' and spares.[13] The helicopter acquisition, together with other assorted equipment on order, marks a new direction for Myanmar and opens up a potential new market for Russia. It will significantly boost the helicopter inventory of the Myanmar Air Force—currently about 12 Bell 205s, 6 Bell 206s, 9 SA-316s, 10 Mi-2s and 12 PZL W-3 Sokols in addition to the 7 Mi-17s obtained in 1995.[14]

Some experts suggest that the next phase of Myanmar's military modernization could include two or three frigates and several missile patrol boats for the navy, and a squadron of advanced fighters for the air force. According to some Russian sources, Myanmar may order an unspecified number of MiG-29s to enhance its air force capabilities.[15] The army's interest is thought to focus on artillery and engineering equipment. However, analysts are sceptical about Myanmar's ability to fund such ambitious programmes in its current circumstances. This could change in the near future when revenue begins to flow from exports from the natural gas deposits in the Gulf of Martaban, now being developed.[16]

The Russian–Myanmar defence ties were viewed negatively by the West, particularly the USA, and by Japan, mainly because of the human rights record in Myanmar and its alleged involvement in drug trafficking.[17] The USA, the European Union and Japan asked ASEAN to delay Myanmar's entry into ASEAN until the military regime which seized power in 1988 improved its human rights record and eased political repression. In May 1997 the US Administration banned all new US investment in Myanmar, citing increased political abuses in the country and its continued production of opium and heroin, much of which is smuggled to the West. US Secretary of State Madeleine Albright wrote to various ASEAN leaders to persuade them to delay Myanmar's entry. Japan also expressed concern that early membership for Myanmar could be seen as support for its mili-

---

[13] *Jane's Defence Weekly,* 4 Sep. 1996, p. 19.

[14] International Institute for Strategic Studies, *The Military Balance 1996/97* (Oxford University Press: Oxford, 1996), p. 164.

[15] Butowski, P., 'Thrust-vectoring will drive MiG-29 exports', *Jane's Defence Weekly,* 21 May 1997, p. 28.

[16] *Jane's Defence Weekly,* 4 Sep. 1996, p. 19.

[17] *The Economist,* 3 May 1997, pp. 15–16, and 7 June 1997, pp. 69–70.

tary government.[18] ASEAN, however, did not take these concerns into consideration, and Myanmar was admitted to the Association in July 1997. This was a clear message to Russia that it can ignore US, EU and Japanese discontent with Myanmar's military regime.

III. Laos

Laos enjoyed close defence relations with Russia and Viet Nam until the early 1990s, when domestic problems forced the latter two countries to focus on internal issues. This encouraged Laos to seek closer ties with China, with which it signed a military cooperation agreement in late 1993. Laotian concerns about becoming too reliant on China subsequently coincided with Russia's efforts to redefine its relations with its traditional allies.

At least two attempts to finalize a defence-related memorandum of understanding failed because of disagreement on the terms of payment. Finally, Laos and Russia signed a long-delayed military cooperation agreement in late 1996, although there has been no public announcement of the agreement. No details are available of how the payment dispute was resolved or what type of equipment and training the Laotian Government was seeking from Russia. Some accounts suggested that, together with arms sales and training, the agreement included Russian assistance in setting up Laos' first defence industries. This could eventually lead to the establishment of facilities to produce ammunition and spare parts, perhaps for artillery and armoured vehicles.[19]

After Myanmar's acquisitions, Laos also ordered 12 Mi-17B helicopters from Russia in late 1997.

IV. Malaysia

For various reasons, such as the country's economic prosperity, its need to replace old armaments, tensions with the USA over arms export and human rights issues, and a desire to diversify its sources of

---

[18] Richardson, M., 'Voting for Burma, ASEAN aims at unity in its region', *International Herald Tribune,* 2 June 1997, p. 4.

[19] Karniol, R., 'Laos seeks industrial spin-off in Russian pact', *Jane's Defence Weekly,* 29 Jan. 1997, p. 14.

weaponry, Malaysia was from the beginning an interesting market for Russia.

In 1992 Russia offered Malaysia MiG-29 aircraft and Mil Mi-35P attack helicopters. In initial talks with the Malaysian Government, the Russian package consisted of 16 MiG-29M operational fighters, 2 MiG-29M/UM operational conversion trainers, 1 flight simulator for the MiG-29M, 6 Mi-35P helicopters and 1 cockpit simulator for the Mi-35P. There was also an upgrade package for the MiG-29M/UM, under separate funding, which included improvements to the time between engine overhauls and to engine lifetime, avionics and systems integration and installation of an air-to-air refuelling probe.[20]

Russia sought to establish links between buyers of its arms. India signed its first defence cooperation agreement with an ASEAN state with Malaysia[21] and has the capability to build, operate and maintain the MiG-29. It could therefore supply Malaysia with spares as part of its own technology and production agreements with Russia, and thereby establish a network of arms buyers and producers. The Malaysian deal included from the beginning a training package for the Royal Malaysian Air Force (RMAF) teams in India for both the MiG-29M/UM and the Mi-35P.

Then Russian Vice-President Alexander Rutskoy noted that Russia was ready to enter into shipbuilding, high-technology, conversion and space technology deals with Malaysia and the ASEAN nations to help Malaysia launch its own telecommunications satellite. He also proposed building factories in Malaysia to refit and modernize 5000 decommissioned An-12 transport aircraft (a proposal which was never realized).[22]

However, very soon Russian–Malaysian talks on arms sales began to be complicated by differences over payment. After difficult negotiations, Russia again accepted partial payment in barter (palm oil and textiles) for the MiG-29 deal.[23] Moreover, Russia had to reduce its price to 20 per cent of its initial offer to demonstrate its flexibility.[24]

Malaysia exemplified the competition between Russian and US arms producers. There were reports in connection with the MiG-29

[20] *Asian Military Review*, Aug.–Sep. 1993, p. 16.

[21] A memorandum of understanding was signed in 1993. *Jane's Defence Weekly*, 9 Dec. 1995, p. 12.

[22] Blank (note 11), p. 62.

[23] According to some Russian sources, the barter part of the deal amounted to 25%. Litovkin (note 10), p. 3.

[24] Blank (note 11), p. 62.

sale that a Russian–US commission led by Russian Prime Minister Chernomyrdin and US Vice-President Albert Gore had been set up to regulate, among other questions, relations in arms sale policy.[25] An agreement between the two governments was reached to allow Russia to sell conventional arms to 'non-terrorist' states in exchange for renouncing the sale of weapons of mass destruction and 'other high-class weapons' to 'irresponsible regimes'. Malaysia was to be the test case for Russian entry into the ASEAN market. However, under pressure from McDonnell-Douglas and General Dynamics, the US Government lobbied Malaysia to choose US fighters, even forcing the US firms to reduce their prices by 30 per cent. British Aerospace also joined in the competition. A compromise decision was taken by the Malaysian Government in 1994. It decided to purchase both 18 MiG-29s and 8 McDonnell-Douglas F/A-18Ds. This settled the Russian–US rivalry to some extent.

The final version of the MiG-29 deal included 16 MiG-29Ns, 2 two-seater MiG-29NUBs and 2 additional MiG-29NUBs for ground personnel training. Along with the Russian part of the contract ($550 million), the deal included Indian training, British avionics retrofit and Canadian simulator packages.[26] The MiG-29s, which have flown from the RMAF Kuantan base since mid-1995, attained operational status in early 1996, replacing the F-5E in the air defence role. The agreement also included a four-part improvement programme. Upgrading of the MiG-29s should cover fitting the in-flight refuelling system, increasing combat load to 3 tonnes, integration of the active radar-guided Vympel RVV-AE (R-77) AAM, and installation of the Phazotron Zhuk radar to enable twin-target engagement at beyond visual range.[27]

According to one observer, the RMAF's interest in developing a mid-air refuelling capability aimed at balancing neighbouring Singapore's fleet of four Lockheed KC-135A Stratotankers, supplemented by the acquisition of four KC-130B and one KC-130H

[25] The US–Russian Joint Commission on Economic and Technological Cooperation (Gore–Chernomyrdin Commission) was established in 1993 to promote cooperation on a wide range of issues related to i.a. science and technology and defence conversion. See, e.g., Anthony, I. and Zanders, J. P., 'Multilateral security-related export controls', *SIPRI Yearbook 1998: Armaments, Disarmament and International Security* (Oxford University Press: Oxford, 1998), pp. 397, 427.

[26] *Asian Military Review*, Aug.–Sep. 1993, p. 16; and *Asian Defence Journal*, Dec. 1995, p. 58.

[27] *Jane's Defence Weekly,* 28 Feb. 1996, p. 4.

tanker/transports in 1996.[28] Indonesia has a similar capability, with two KC-130B tankers in its air force inventory.[29] MiG-MAPO started in November 1995 and completed in early 1996 an in-flight refuelling trial on a 'standard' Russian MiG-29. Tests were carried out at altitudes of up to 26 000 ft (7926 m) and speeds of 400–600 km/h behind an Il-78 Midas tanker. Tests were also made at speeds of 350–500 km/h to simulate the flight characteristics of a KC-130 tanker. The Malaysian Ministry of Defence was satisfied with the results.[30] According to MAPO officials, the packages were due to be installed in 1996.

Malaysia's six C-130 Hercules transport aircraft were to be converted into dual-role transport–tankers.[31] Speaking in January 1997 at a training school ceremony in Ipoh, Lieutenant-General Datuk Ahmad Saruji Che Rose, Commander-in-Chief of the RMAF, said that one C-130 transport had already been converted and that another was due to undergo the same process. Lockheed Martin Aeronautical Support Systems provided kits to modify two C-130Hs to the tanker role. Modification work was done by Malaysia's Airod.[32] According to some Russian sources, the RMAF was pleased with the performance of in-flight refuelling technology in the Flying Fish-97 exercise, which was conducted in April 1997 by the air forces and navies of Australia, Malaysia, New Zealand, Singapore and the UK in the South China Sea.[33]

Acquisition of in-flight refuelling technology will certainly make Malaysia a more influential regional player than before. This programme may be aimed at balancing not only similar capabilities of the neighbouring ASEAN countries but also China's growing influence in South-East Asia.

Malaysia also asked for adaptation of the airframe and equipment for wet, tropical climate conditions; installation of satellite communications and navigation systems; and extension of the service lifetime of the RD-33 engine, taking it up to 2000 hours before the first major overhaul. The service life of RD-33 Series 2 engines is 700 hours

---

[28] Karniol, R., 'Malaysia chases others in refuelling capability', *Jane's Defence Weekly*, 22 Jan. 1997, p. 12. According to *The Military Balance 1996/97* (note 14), p. 198, Singapore has 4 KC-130Bs, 5 C-130Hs and 1 KC-130H but no KC-135A.

[29] *The Military Balance 1996/97* (note 14), p. 184.

[30] *Jane's Defence Weekly,* 28 Feb. 1996, p. 4.

[31] Butowski (note 15), p. 29.

[32] Karniol (note 27), p. 12.

[33] *Rossiyskaya Gazeta,* 20 May 1997, p. 7.

between major overhauls and 1400 hours for total service life and 1000 and 2000 hours, respectively, for RD-33 Series 3 engines.[34]

Considerable effort has also been expended in improving engineering support for the RMAF, in part by taking advantage of the offset provisions of current procurement programmes. As part of the $220 million in offsets in the MiG-29 package, in 1995 Rosvooruzheniye and MiG-MAPO helped the Malaysian Government to establish the joint venture Aerospace Technology System Corporation (ATSC), which was responsible for maintenance and overhaul of RMAF ground support equipment as well as for operating a regional service centre for MiG-29s.[35] On 16 October 1997 the two countries signed a $34.4 million contract on an upgrading programme. Two upgraded MiG-29s were delivered to the RMAF in May 1998, at the opening ceremony of this regional service centre and modernization of 16 other aircraft was due by the end of 1998.[36]

Some money from the Malaysian contract was used by the Russian party to start production of the R-77 AAM. Development work on this missile, the Russian counterpart to the US AIM-120 advanced medium-range air-to-air missile (AMRAAM) which the USA has been reluctant to supply to the region, had been going on for 15 years, but when it was completed there was no money for production. By ordering the R-77 for its MiG-29s Malaysia effectively underwrote its serial production. R-77 production was originally planned for the Arsenal works at Kiev in Ukraine. According to Anatoliy Belosvet, first deputy director of the MiG-MAPO company, a MiG-29 equipped with R-77 missiles will have six to seven times more capability in beyond-visual-range combat than an aircraft equipped with R-27 (AA-10 Alamo) or AIM-7 Sparrow missiles.[37]

In addition to enhancing its air force capabilities, with the Russian aircraft Malaysia obtained another item of leverage to press the United States on arms trade issues. Responding in June 1995 to suggestions that the US Congress might block the sale of these aircraft to Malaysia following allegations of human rights violations, Prime Minister Mohamed Mahathir said that the purchase of extra MiG-29s

<hr>

[34] Butowski (note 15), p. 29.
[35] *Asian Defence Journal*, Dec. 1995, p. 63.
[36] *Nezavisimoye Voyennoye Obozreniye*, 19–25 Dec. 1997, p. 2, and 15–21 May 1998, p. 3.
[37] Butowski (note 15), p. 29.

instead of the F/A-18s was an option.[38] The F/A-18s were delivered in early 1997. General Richard Robless, director of the ATSC, also expressed interest in the new Russian MiG-AT trainer being developed by MiG-MAPO.[39]

In accordance with the Seventh Malaysian Plan, covering development spending over the period 1996–2000, the RMAF plans to acquire 12–24 attack helicopters. The current preferences are the South African Atlas CSH-2 Rooivalk and the McDonnell-Douglas AH-64D Apache, but the Apache may not be an option since the US Government is not likely to approve its sale to South-East Asian customers for at least another three or four years. Other options include the Russian Mil Mi-28 and Mi-35 and the Kamov Ka-50.[40]

A longer-term RMAF requirement is for 10–16 additional F/A-18Ds or MiG-29s. According to some accounts, Malaysia was close to deciding to buy a second batch of 18 MiG-29s.[41] However, bearing in mind the RMAF's other requirements and the need to evaluate the in-service performance of both Russian and US fighter types before making a decision, it seems unlikely that funds for such a purchase will be made available before the eighth national five-year plan (2001–2005).

In December 1995 Defence Minister Dato Syed Hamid Albar said that Malaysia would acquire some MBTs. The requirement was said to stem from considerations of future UN peacekeeping service for which Malaysia will have to have the 'necessary equipment'. Along with the T-72 (offered by Poland and Slovakia) and the UK's Vickers Mk III, Russia's T-72S emerged as a potential bidder in mid-1996.[42]

V. Indonesia

Most of Indonesia's military equipment is from the USA or Europe. In 1996 Indonesia decided to continue the modernization of its air force by acquiring 9 US F-16 and 16 British Hawk fighter aircraft. However, in early 1997 both the USA and the UK had become critical of Indonesia's human rights record. The British Labour Government

[38] *Asian Defence Journal*, Dec. 1995, p. 58.
[39] *Nezavisimoye Voyennoye Obozreniye*, 19–25 Dec. 1997, p. 2.
[40] *Asian Defence Journal*, Dec. 1995, p. 62.
[41] Butowski (note 15), p. 28.
[42] Cloughley, B., 'Malaysia strains for a greater world standing', *Jane's International Defense Review*, Apr. 1997, p. 22.

confirmed in July 1997 that the Hawk contract with Indonesia would go ahead but unveiled new rules to halt arms sales to regimes that might use British-made weapons for internal suppression or external aggression. This made the prospects for future British military contracts with Indonesia doubtful.

In June 1997 Indonesia cancelled a plan to buy F-16s from the USA because of what it said was 'wholly unjustified criticism' in the US Congress of its human rights record, particular in East Timor. Indonesia also pulled out of a US government-funded military education and training programme.

After two months of negotiations with Russia, in early August 1997 Indonesia announced its decision to buy 12 Su-30K fighters for the air force and 8 Mi-17-1B troop transport helicopters for the army's elite commando forces. Part of the $500 million purchase would be a barter arrangement to exchange commodities such as palm oil, coffee and rubber for the aircraft.[43] While Indonesia wanted 20 of the fighters 'for the first phase, [it] decided on eight helicopters and 12 fighter planes'[44] and indicated that Russia would probably get subsequent arms orders. Indonesia should be the second country, after India, to receive the advanced Su-30K fighter, which is considered superior to the Su-27 that China and Viet Nam have acquired from Russia. The Su-30K can fly at twice the speed of sound and has a combat range of 3000 km, about three times that of an F-16 without aerial refuelling.[45] It is well suited to long-range patrol and interception missions in Indonesia, an archipelago of over 17 000 islands stretching over 5000 km.

The political implications of the Su-30K deal, however, were much more important than the military ones. Indonesia's decision to turn to Russia was a serious setback for the US and European defence industries' efforts to keep their positions in the growing but competitive East Asian arms market. Russian military analysts predict that other customers in the region, such as Japan, the Philippines, Thailand, Singapore and South Korea, may start buying Russian weapon systems, which are cheaper than comparable Western equipment.[46]

[43] Yusin, M., 'Moskva zakreplyaetsya na oruzheynom rynke ASEAN' [Moscow consolidates its hold on the ASEAN arms market], *Izvestiya*, 6 Aug. 1997, p. 3.

[44] Richardson, M., 'Slap at US as Russia gets Jakarta fighter deal', *International Herald Tribune*, 6 Aug. 1997, p. 1.

[45] Richardson (note 44), p. 2.

[46] Litovkin (note 10), p. 3.

Some Russian sources suggest that Indonesia also decided to order a number of Russian BMP-3 infantry combat vehicles (ICVs) and BTR-80A APCs.[47] Indonesia's armed forces has also shown interest in Russian radars and missiles for a planned major upgrade of the country's air defence system. Military–technical cooperation between Indonesia and Russia suffered from the financial crisis in South-East Asia of 1997–98 and the collapse of the Suharto regime in the spring of 1998, and realization of the above contracts has been postponed for an indefinite period.

VI. Singapore

Since 1993 Singapore has shown interest in Russian missile systems. It was briefed by Russia on the SS-21 Scarab SSM in early 1993.[48] The SS-21 (Russian designation Tochka) is a short-range, road-mobile, solid-propellant, single-warhead ballistic missile or OTR-21 system using the 9M79 missile. With a maximum payload of 482 kg and estimated range of 150 km, it falls below the Missile Technology Control Regime (MTCR) limit of 500-kg payload and 300-km range.[49] No South-East Asian country has SSMs in its inventory.

The unpublicized 1993 meeting between defence officials from Russia and Singapore was the first such contact. Similar talks have since been held between Russian industry and the Singapore military. There has been no follow-up to the 1993 meeting, but in early 1996 Singapore expressed interest in Russia's S-300 air defence system. This system is significantly more sophisticated than others in the region. However, some experts maintain that Singapore has traditionally been careful about being seen as the first country to introduce new military technologies to South-East Asia.[50] Singapore is therefore not likely to acquire the S-300 SAM system before other countries acquire similar systems.

In late 1997 Singapore bought other, less destabilizing systems— SA-16 or SA-18 shoulder-launched SAMs—from Russia.

---

[47] Klenov, V., 'Nashi voyennye sekrety dlya NATO: zachem?' [Our military secrets for NATO: why?], *Rossiyskaya Gazeta*, 25 Sep. 1997, p. 5.

[48] *Jane's Defence Weekly*, 4 Sep. 1996, p. 3.

[49] For a description of the MTCR, see Anthony, I. and Zanders, J. P., 'Multilateral security-related export controls', *SIPRI Yearbook 1998: Armaments, Disarmament and International Security* (Oxford University Press: Oxford, 1998), pp. 394–99.

[50] *Jane's Defence Weekly*, 4 Sep. 1996, p. 3.

VII. Thailand

Thailand has expressed interest in military–technical cooperation with Russia in connection with its modernization plans. According to Marshal M. R. Siripong Thongyai, Commander-in-Chief of the Royal Thai Air Force (RTAF), apart from buying F/A-18s the RTAF would consider purchasing other jet fighters, including the MiG-29, the Su-27 and the Su-35.[51] This decision was partly provoked by the USA's initial reluctance to supply AIM-120 AMRAAMs for the RTAF's 36-aircraft F-16 fleet.[52] The USA finally approved the sale, but the RTAF was dissatisfied with the US delay.

The RTAF's eagerness to acquire a new fighter and its insistence on the AMRAAM was partly spurred on by Malaysia's purchase of the MiG-29 and F-18D and Viet Nam's order for the Su-27. Russia is also understood to be supplying each of the countries with export variants of the R-77 (AA-12 Adder) AMRAAM.[53] Russian and US transfers of advanced weapon systems to the neighbouring countries provoked a new round of the regional arms race.

The Thai Navy is seeking four submarines under its 1997–2001 military development plan. Among the types mentioned as possibilities, along with German, Italian, Spanish and Swedish types, is the Russian Kilo Class.[54]

In 1996 the Royal Thai Army declared its intention to buy up to 295 armoured fighting vehicles (AFVs). Thailand initially decided to choose the French GIAT Industries' VAB 6 x 6 APC but encountered protests from a number of manufacturers. As a result of the protests it reopened its competition for an AFV and issued invitations to nine manufacturers to send their vehicles to Thailand for trials. Among the companies invited is the Russian Nizhniy Novgorod Automobile Plant, producer of the GAZ BTR-80 8 x 8 AFV. Trials were scheduled to take place in June–July 1997.[55]

---

[51] *Asian Defence Journal*, Dec. 1995, p. 131.

[52] *Asian Defence Journal*, Mar. 1996, p. 83.

[53] *Strategic Digest*, Nov. 1995, p. 172.

[54] *Asian Defence Journal*, Jan. 1996, p. 65; and Kotelkin, A., 'Russia and the world arms market', *International Affairs* (Moscow), vol. 42, no. 4 (1996), p. 36.

[55] Foss, C. F., 'Thailand to reopen APC contest after protests', *Jane's Defence Weekly*, 19 Feb. 1997, p. 13.

There were also unconfirmed reports that Russia had offered to trade 20 Mi-17B military helicopters to Thailand to help settle its $65 million debt for rice purchases.[56]

VIII. Viet Nam

It is now more than 20 years since Viet Nam was reunited under communist rule. It is not surprising that its aircraft are predominantly of Soviet design, but newer or modernized types, such as Su-27 and MiG-23 fighter aircraft and Mi-24 helicopters, are now being acquired from Russia.[57] In particular, Viet Nam decided in 1995 to acquire 12 Su-27s. At the same time it preferred to work with Israel, not Russia, on the upgrade of some of its 150 MiG-21 fighters.[58] According to the source, this was a programme, not merely plans. Viet Nam is believed to have paid 85 per cent of the Su-27 price in hard currency and the rest by barter in agricultural products.[59]

Arms transfers were formerly accompanied by an enhancement of the overall Russian military presence in a country. For instance, Russia stepped up military contacts with Viet Nam in 1995 and asked if its navy could expand its operations at Cam Ranh Bay, according to a Vietnamese military source. Russia maintains a small naval operation at the former US base. Hanoi is said to have turned down a secret US request to allow US ships to visit the naval base.[60]

Meanwhile, Viet Nam fostered its cooperation with Russia in order to develop a navy of its own. Its interest in increasing its naval capabilities stems mainly from its concerns about the South China Sea, where its claim to the Spratly islands is contested by Brunei, China, Malaysia, the Philippines and Taiwan. In 1988 Chinese forces seized five reefs in the Spratlys from Viet Nam after sinking several Vietnamese support craft. Tensions in the area escalated in 1995, when China occupied a reef claimed by the Philippines.[61]

In 1996 two Tarantul-1 Class FACs were delivered to Viet Nam by Russia. The craft, each armed with four SS-N-2 'Styx' SSM launch-

---

[56] Hull, A. and Markov, D., 'Trends in the arms market', *Jane's Intelligence Review*, May 1997, p. 234.

[57] *Asian Defence Journal*, Feb. 1996, p. 42.

[58] *Far Eastern Economic Review*, 21 Mar. 1996, p. 24.

[59] *Jane's Intelligence Review*, Sep. 1995, p. 3.

[60] *Jane's International Defense Review*, Feb. 1997, p. 13.

[61] *Jane's Intelligence Review*, Sep. 1995, p. 3.

ers, represented a significant upgrading of the Vietnamese Navy's potential for operations in the South China Sea.[62]

Two new missile craft designed by the Severnoye Design Bureau in Russia for the Vietnamese Navy are under construction at a yard in Ho Chi Minh City, using sections built in Russia. The acquisition of these vessels will increase (if modestly) the capabilities of the Vietnamese Navy and at least help to maintain the fleet at a level comparable to those of neighbouring countries such as Cambodia, Indonesia, Laos, Malaysia, the Philippines, Singapore and Thailand. At the same time, Viet Nam is unable to compete with other regional sea powers, such as China, Japan, South Korea and Taiwan.

Viet Nam was also considering buying fast patrol boats and corvettes from Russia to bolster its naval capability in the South China Sea.[63]

In summary, despite the traditional exporters' resistance, Russia has succeeded in penetrating the ASEAN arms market by establishing military–technical cooperation with new partners and by redefining its defence ties with former allies. However, it is unlikely that major arms suppliers such as France, Germany, the UK and the USA will give up their efforts in this market. Continuing competition between Russia and Western countries can be confidently predicted in the years to come.

[62] *Jane's Intelligence Review*, Sep. 1995, p. 3.
[63] *Far Eastern Economic Review*, 28 Dec. 1995–4 Jan. 1996, p. 14.

6. North and South Korea

I. Introduction

Since the break-up of the Soviet Union, Russia has faced a serious challenge to its diplomacy on the Korean peninsula. On the one hand, North Korea (the Democratic People's Republic of Korea) was a traditional ally of the Soviet Union from the late 1940s. Unlike Russia, North Korea did not want to do away with the socialist regime or reform it and ease tensions with South Korea (the Republic of Korea). On the other hand, Russia was eager to establish diplomatic and economic relations with South Korea in order to attract South Korean investment to the troubled Russian economy.

The Russian domestic debate has resulted in a so-called 'even-handed' policy towards the two Korean states. As Russian diplomats and academics emphasize, Russian national interests are best served by détente and dialogue; a constructive, complementary partnership with South Korea; and good-neighbourly, mutually advantageous relations with North Korea. They stress that Russia proceeds from these premises in its Korean policy rather than from the traditional balance-of-power principle: Russia is not developing its ties with one Korean state at the expense of those with the other.[1]

In reality, however, Russia's policy towards the Korean peninsula has not always been even-handed or ruled by a cooperative security paradigm. Rather, Russia has used traditional realpolitik diplomatic instruments such as containment, hard negotiation tactics, maintenance of the regional military balance and aggressive arms sale policies. Sometimes its regional policy has been driven by purely economic considerations to the detriment of conflict resolution and regional security. As with South-East Asia, Russia has been eager to remain an important regional player, although some other countries favour a more limited Russian role.

II. North Korea

The former USSR, along with China, was instrumental in installing the communist regime in North Korea after World War II and pro-

[1] Moiseyev, V., 'Russia and the Korean peninsula', *International Affairs* (Moscow), vol. 42, no. 1 (1996), pp. 106–107.

vided it with military support during the Korean War. The two countries included formal provisions for automatic military intervention in the event of attack by a third country in their 1961 Treaty of Friendship, Cooperation and Mutual Assistance. After the mid-1960s the USSR delivered arms worth 3.3 billion roubles to North Korea, including MiG-23 and MiG-29 fighters, T-72 main battle tanks (MBTs), various surface-to-air missiles, helicopters and small arms. More than half of the combat equipment of the North Korean Army was Soviet-made.[2]

At the end of the 1980s North Korea concluded a contract with the USSR to buy 100 MiG-29s, having received about 30 MiG-29s in the mid-1980s.[3] Although none of the 100 aircraft was delivered, North Korea succeeded in assembling two MiG-29s in 1992.[4]

Rapprochement with South Korea, however, started in 1991 and has been accompanied by worsening relations with North Korea, in particular the cutting of defence ties between the two countries. By mid-1992 Russian officials were claiming openly that they would not supply North Korea with weapon systems or technical assistance for military purposes and that Russia opposed the nuclearization of the Korean peninsula. When President Yeltsin visited Seoul in November 1992 he denounced the 1961 treaty, strongly suggesting that Russia would no longer honour the pledge to defend the North in a war, cut off military aid, and 'impose political pressure' on North Korea to stop its nuclear weapon programme.[5] The treaty officially expired in 1996; no new treaty has been concluded so far, although they have declared their intention to conclude one. According to some reports, a new basic agreement on relations between Russia and North Korea could be reached in the near future, to include renewed military cooperation but exclude a military intervention clause. The first round of talks on a new agreement, held in Pyongyang on 21–24 January 1997, made 'considerable progress', according to Russian accounts.[6]

---

[2] For a comprehensive account of Russian arms deliveries to North Korea, see Kirshin, Yu., 'Conventional arms transfers during the Soviet period', ed. I. Anthony, SIPRI, *Russia and the Arms Trade* (Oxford University Press: Oxford, 1998), pp. 48–60.

[3] International Institute for Strategic Studies, *The Military Balance 1996/97* (Oxford University Press: Oxford, 1996), p. 187.

[4] Cohen, J. and Peach, A., 'The spread of advanced aircraft', ed. R. Forsberg, *The Arms Production Dilemma* (MIT Press: Cambridge, Mass., 1994), p. 251.

[5] Reid, T. R., 'Moscow, Seoul forge new relationship', *Washington Post,* 21 Nov. 1992, p. A6.

[6] *Jane's Defence Weekly,* 29 Jan. 1997, p. 14.

Russian Deputy Foreign Minister Grigoriy Karasin, who headed the Russian delegation, said that it would include provisions 'establishing absolutely normal military and technical cooperation with North Korea'. In an interview on Russian television he also said that the cooperation would include supply of weapons and spare parts, training and military exchanges. The only constraints, he added, were that cooperation should not contravene Russia's international commitments or upset the military balance on the Korean peninsula.[7]

The age of North Korea's armaments is one likely reason why it would like to resume its military ties with Russia. Five North Korean military aircraft crashed in 1996, according to a South Korean Defence Ministry official: one Mi-2 helicopter in March, a MiG-19 fighter in September, a MiG-21 in October and two MiG-21s in December.[8] The fact that North Korea is cut off from arms supplies and would buy weapons and military technologies from anyone who offered them is another reason for the resumption of military–technical cooperation between North Korea and Russia.

Some reports suggest that in the future North Korea may be able to produce MiG-29s under Russian licence. It could conceivably buy or produce under licence up to 25 MiG-29s by the year 2000 in an effort to begin replacing the obsolete J-5s, J-6s, MiG-21s and MiG-23s which make up the greater part of its combat aircraft inventory.[9]

Long before its collapse, the USSR developed cooperative training and nuclear- and weapons-related trade relations with some developing countries, including North Korea. Soviet relations with North Korea in the nuclear field date back to the 1950s, when training was provided for North Korean scientists at the Joint Institute for Nuclear Research in Dubna, Russia. This cooperation was crucial for the development of North Korea's first nuclear test reactor in 1963. Many Western and Asia–Pacific nations are now concerned with the 'brain drain' of former Soviet scientists with expertise in R&D and production of weapons of mass destruction. Economic reform, hyperinflation and cuts in science spending have contributed to economic and social hardship for Russian scientists, resulting in an exodus of scientific knowledge, and Soviet-era travel restrictions have been relaxed. Moreover, the opening of the former Soviet borders has

---

[7] *Jane's Defence Weekly,* 19 Feb. 1997, p. 12.
[8] *Jane's Defence Weekly,* 22 Jan. 1997, p. 12.
[9] Cohen and Peach (note 4), p. 251.

enabled foreign governments and private companies to establish trade offices in Russia. There have been regular reports since 1991 that countries such as China, India, Iran, Iraq, North Korea, Pakistan and Turkey have been actively seeking the cooperation of Russian scientists and weapon experts.

In 1992 the US Central Intelligence Agency, the Russian Ministry of Atomic Energy (Minatom) and the German Federal Intelligence Service all published estimates that up to 3000 former Soviet nuclear scientists either had detailed knowledge of nuclear weapon design or had mastered the technology for producing nuclear weapons.[10] According to another CIA estimate, some 900 000 people in the former USSR, civilian as well as military, had clearances to work with nuclear weapons. Of these, 2000 had detailed knowledge of weapon design and 3000–5000 worked at a high level in the production of fissile material.[11] Glenn E. Schweitzer, former executive director of the International Science and Technology Center in Moscow, suggested in 1996 that 60 000 Russian 'core specialists' had the experience and expertise that could interest countries involved in clandestine programmes for weapons of mass destruction. Of these, 30 000 were from the aerospace industry, 20 000 from the nuclear industry and 10 000 from the chemical and biological weapon industries.[12] According to some more sceptical estimates, only 100–200 individuals actually had the full range of knowledge about how to design, develop, manufacture and field nuclear weapons.[13]

Contrary to some simplistic assessments, most such specialists are under rigid control of the Russian security services. For example, a recent Russian press report suggested that the Russian Federal Security Service had identified and was monitoring a 'core group' of such specialists. On one occasion, a group of 36 Russian scientists from the Makeyev Design Bureau (which designs submarine-launched ballistic missiles) was stopped at Moscow's Sheremetyevo Airport en route to North Korea in late 1992.[14] Two North Korean officials were

[10] Moody, R. A., 'Armageddon for hire', *Jane's International Defense Review*, Feb. 1997, p. 21.

[11] De Andreis, M. and Calogero, F., *The Soviet Nuclear Weapon Legacy*, SIPRI Research Report no. 10 (Oxford University Press: Oxford, 1995), pp. 47–48.

[12] Moody (note 10), p. 21.

[13] De Andreis and Calogero (note 11), p. 48.

[14] Hull, A. and Markov, D., 'Trends in the arms market', *Jane's Intelligence Review*, May 1997), p. 233.

deported.[15] On another occasion, North Korea tried unsuccessfully to entice 100 Russian rocket engineers to Pyongyang under the guise of official scientific exchanges. Russian intelligence officials claimed that the real purpose was to modernize Scud-C missiles.[16] The country does maintain a cadre of about 10 scientists in Dubna. Russian specialists, some of whom have changed their names to disguise their identity, have been reported to be working in North Korean laboratories.[17]

III. South Korea

Rapprochement with South Korea in both the political and the military areas also started under President Mikhail Gorbachev in 1991. Then Russian Foreign Minister Yevgeniy Primakov, a top-ranking member of the Soviet Academy of Sciences and Chairman of the Supreme Soviet of the Soviet Union, was one of the most active initiators of this rapprochement.[18] Russia regarded South Korea as a profitable trade and economic partner as well as a counterweight to Japan.[19] In 1995 Russian–South Korean trade accounted for $3.3 billion and remained at this level in 1996–97.[20] Russian diplomats and experts commented that Russia's interests were stability on the peninsula, coordinated reductions of weapon supplies, the curtailing of third-country military activities on the peninsula, and US withdrawal in order to foster inter-Korean dialogue and confidence building.

Military issues were from the beginning at the heart of Russian–South Korean relations. In April 1991 it was revealed that Russia had offered MiG-29 and MiG-31 aircraft to South Korea, the former at lower than usual prices, in return for consumer goods. In August 1992 South Korea announced its intention to ask Russia for permission to supply facilities related to commercializing the Russian defence industry and stated that it was considering buying some Russian defence firms in order to operate them as joint ventures. Later it was

[15] Moody (note 10), p. 22.

[16] Hull and Markov (note 14), p. 233.

[17] Moody (note 10), p. 22.

[18] *Literaturnaya Gazeta,* no. 45 (6 Nov. 1996), p. 14.

[19] *Rossiyskaya Gazeta,* 26 Apr. 1997, p. 3.

[20] Kutakov, V., 'Druzhit, sotrudnichat, ukreplyat bezopasnost' [Be friends, cooperate, enhance security], *Rossiyskaya Gazeta,* 25 Apr. 1998, p. 7; and *Literaturnaya Gazeta,* no. 45 (6 Nov. 1996), p. 14.

reported that those ventures were in aerospace, advanced materials, electronics, lasers and genetic engineering. The Russian and South Korean defence industries established some scientific and discussion links to review the joint projects. South Koreans made visits to secret defence plants and were optimistic about the joint projects. South Korean firms were particularly interested in acquiring aerospace technology, including composite materials for aircraft. It was also reported that South Korea was considering buying MiG-29s, mines, torpedoes, tank ammunition, and SA-6, SA-8 and SA-16 SAMs. Russia was also willing to sell space technology and even nuclear technology in line with South Korean interest in producing fissionable materials. Soon afterwards it was announced that a Korean consortium would build the Almaz S-300PMU anti-tactical ballistic missile system and its associated radars under licence.[21] This production should fulfil South Korea's aim of countering North Korea's Scud ballistic missile. No information is available as to the outcome.

Other reports suggested that South Korea would like to buy some S-300PMUs, but the USA has strongly opposed these plans because of concerns about inter-operability. The concern was that the S-300PMU does not have an identification friend-or-foe system compatible with US and Western technologies. During his visit to Japan in April 1997, US Defence Secretary William Cohen said that the USA would prefer a situation in which not a large number of Russian SAMs were actually deployed. However, he said that the USA would not mind if South Korea bought some S-300PMUs 'for testing purposes or other kinds of training'.[22] Cohen pressed South Korea to buy the Patriot air defence system instead of the Russian SAMs.

In November 1992 the two countries signed a military cooperation agreement by which they were to start direct military contacts (exchange of military delegations, visits of navy units, and so on).[23] However, at that stage cooperation did not make any essential progress. Defence ties between Russia and South Korea have been stimulated by a rather unusual factor.

[21] Blank, S. J., *Challenging the New World Order: The Arms Transfers Policies of the Russian Republic* (Strategic Studies Institute, US Army War College: Carlisle Barracks, Pa., 1993), p. 64.

[22] 'USA urges S. Korea to buy Patriot over S-300V', *Jane's Defence Weekly*, 16 Apr. 1997, p. 3.

[23] ITAR-TASS, 22 Nov. 1992; and Miasnikov, V., 'Russian–South Korean security cooperation', *Korean Journal of Defense Analysis*, vol. 6, no. 2 (winter 1994), p. 329.

In 1991 South Korea lent the then Soviet Union $1.47 billion as part of an effort to develop relations with its former adversary. Being unable to repay its debt, Russia offered to trade weapons for debt forgiveness. According to South Korea's semi-official Yonhap News Agency, the government (over the objections of its senior defence officials) concluded that it had 'no choice but to accept the offer' while Russia's foreign debt kept on rising.[24] In April 1995 a barter deal was reached to cover the first $450.7 million in principal and interest. Nearly half that sum, $208.81 million, was in military hardware, largely for intelligence evaluation and training purposes, with delivery from 1995 to 1998. It included unknown numbers of T-80U MBTs, BMP-3 AIFVs, AT-7 Saxhorn anti-tank guided missiles and SA-16 Gimlet SAMs. Some sources suggested that the deal covered MiG-29 and S-300 SAMs as well. These reports have not been confirmed.[25] In 1995 an undisclosed number of South Korean Army personnel began a training course in Russia to prepare for the handover, which was to start at the end of 1996.[26] According to Russian sources, there were 30 Koreans in Russian training centres in 1996.[27] Russian military specialists were sent to South Korea as consultants.

Initially, South Korea asked Russia to provide a battalion of 30 T-80U MBTs, 30 BMP-3 AIFVs, several hundred AT-7 Saxhorn anti-tank guided missiles, Metis-M and SA-18 Igla portable anti-aircraft missiles, ammunition, and spare parts. A number of BTR-80 8 x 8 wheeled APCs were also ordered.

Russia had delivered equipment worth $150 million by the end of 1996. The South Korean Army activated its first unit with Russian AIFVs, a mechanized infantry battalion with 30 BMP-3s, on 1 October 1996 and formed its first armoured battalion equipped with Russian MBTs on 1 November.[28] According to *Jane's Defence Weekly*, in early 1997 it received a third shipment of Russian equipment which included 26 T-80Us.[29] In May 1997 it was reported that South Korea would receive a further shipment of BMP-3 ICVs, spares and ammunition worth $31.25 million from Russia during the year.[30]

---

[24] Hull and Markov (note 14), p. 234.
[25] Hull and Markov (note 14), p. 234.
[26] *Jane's Defence Weekly,* 21 Feb. 1996, p. 15.
[27] *Literaturnaya Gazeta,* no. 45 (note 18), p. 14.
[28] *Jane's Defence Weekly,* 6 Nov. 1996, p. 17.
[29] *Jane's Defence Weekly,* 15 Jan. 1997, p. 13.
[30] *Jane's Defence Weekly,* 18 Dec. 1996, p. 11.

South Korea has also shown interest in Russian advanced fighters. According to some accounts the Su-35, or even the Su-37, is one of four aircraft which South Korea has said is in contention for its requirement for acquisition of a new fighter under its F-X modernization programme.[31] Some reports suggest that South Korea is considering a futuristic Russian jet for a major order of 120 fighters to be delivered after 2002.[32]

There were (unconfirmed) reports that in the autumn of 1996 Samsung Aerospace concluded an agreement to produce and market Russia's Mil Mi-26 transport helicopter.[33] The programme was to be initiated in early 1997.

Since Thailand acquired a small aircraft-carrier in March 1997 and China intends to acquire one, South Korea and many other countries of the region are considering the same possibility. It was suggested that South Korea could be competing with India for the Russian 70 000-tonne aircraft-carrier *Admiral Kuznetsov*. Other possibilities were the *Admiral Gorshkov*, which was under repair, or the *Admiral Kuznetsov*'s sister ship *Varyag*, which may have been sold to China.[34]

A small South Korean tea-trading firm which had only $4.5 million in its bank account bought two decommissioned Russian carriers, the *Minsk* and the *Novorossiysk*, for as little as $4.5 million and $4.3 million, respectively, to scrap them along with 200 other Russian ships in Chinese, Korean and Vietnamese ports. Initially, they might have been delivered fully equipped; delivery was due in early 1995. However, the Russian Embassy in Seoul opposed these deals for security reasons. Russian diplomats wondered how a small tea-trading firm was able to strike such a deal. The embassy insisted, successfully in the end, that all military equipment should be taken off the vessels.[35] These minor tensions, however, did not prevent Russian–South Korean defence cooperation.

These developments illustrate South Korea's interest in acquiring an aircraft-carrier or related technology, but with the financial crisis in Asia the plans to acquire an aircraft-carrier seem unrealistic.

[31] *Jane's Defence Weekly,* 6 Nov. 1996, p. 17.

[32] Richardson, M., 'Russia making inroads in Asian arms market', *International Herald Tribune,* 15 Mar. 1997, p. 2; and Richardson, M., 'Slap at US as Russia gets Jakarta fighter deal', *International Herald Tribune,* 6 Aug. 1997, p. 1.

[33] *Jane's Defence Weekly,* 6 Nov. 1996, p. 19.

[34] *Asian Defence Journal,* Jan. 1996, p. 75.

[35] *Literaturnaya Gazeta* (note 18), p. 14.

In October 1996 Lee Bong-hee, head of Daewoo Heavy Industries, said before a South Korean parliamentary committee that South Korea was seeking to develop its own 1800-tonne submarine with Russian assistance. He told legislators that the assistance includes conceptual design and submarine manufacturing technology,[36] but the details of this project have not been disclosed.

In summary, Russian arms sale policies towards the Korean peninsula in the 1990s have a mixed record. Russia has succeeded in establishing military–technical cooperation with South Korea, and its security relations with North Korea have been redefined in a more pragmatic way. At the same time, in contrast with its promises to conduct an 'even-handed' strategy and not violate the military balance in the area, Russia's actual arms transfer policy has been more favourable to South Korea than to North Korea. Moreover, that policy has sometimes been a hostage of technical or economic problems rather than an instrument of a sound security strategy. For instance, military–technical cooperation with South Korea was not one of autonomous bilateral relations but was subordinated to economic and financial considerations. In this context, it remains unclear how Russia will use arms transfers to promote security and stability on the peninsula and to encourage dialogue between the two Korean states with the final aim of their unification. It appears that Russia's short-term and purely pragmatic requirements (such as repayment of debts or obtaining currency) sometimes undermine or distort the long-term objectives of its security policy towards the region.

---

[36] *Jane's Defence Weekly,* 20 Oct. 1996, p. 17; and Richardson (note 32), p. 2.

7. The security implications of Russian arms transfers to East Asia

I. Introduction

Whether or not Russian arms transfers to East Asia are a destabilizing factor for security in the region is open to argument. Russian officials and many analysts claim that they make a positive contribution to security and the military balance in the region, while Western and some East Asian politicians and scholars tend to assess Russian arms sales policy in negative terms.[1] Assessments depend on the analyst's nationality, political preferences and conceptual framework.

Some authors suggest that arms sales are bad, ethically and politically, and have negative effects: they feed local arms races, create or enhance regional instabilities, make wars more violent, and increase the tendency for outside powers to be drawn into conflicts. This group maintains that the trade in arms should be prohibited or limited.[2]

According to another school of thought, arms transfers do not of themselves lead to conflict or war but are a result or side-effect of conflict; to oppose the arms trade is to try to cure the symptoms rather than the illness. The causes of conflict should be addressed and resolved, and if conflict resolution succeeds the demand for arms will diminish or disappear. By giving away or selling arms, this school maintains, the supplier country acquires political influence or friendship and receives economic benefits. It can manage a conflict by providing the weaker partner or victim of aggression with the instruments of resistance and can influence a client's behaviour, preventing aggression or other irresponsible action. Regional peace and stability may be advanced rather than hindered by the transfer of arms.[3]

---

[1] E.g., Blank, S. J., *Challenging the New World Order: The Arms Transfers Policies of the Russian Republic* (Strategic Studies Institute, US Army War College: Carlisle Barracks, Pa., 1993); and Acharya, A., *An Arms Race in Post-Cold War Southeast Asia?: Prospects for Control* (Institute of Southeast Asian Studies: Singapore, 1994).

[2] E.g., Boutwell, J., Klare, M. T. and Reed, L. W. (eds), *Lethal Commerce: The Global Trade in Small Arms and Light Weapons* (American Academy of Arts and Sciences: Cambridge, Mass., 1995), pp. 145–48; and Gülcher, E., *Tackling the Flow of Arms* (International Peace Bureau/International Peace Information Service: Geneva, 1992).

[3] Adeniji, O., 'Restraint as a factor in resolving regional conflicts', United Nations, *Transparency in International Arms Transfers,* Disarmament Topical Papers no. 3 (UN: New York, 1990), p. 103; and Kolodziej, E. A., *Making and Marketing Arms: The French Experience*

The third school of thought points out that supplier-imposed arms transfer controls are resented by the recipients as paternalistic and discriminatory. They can amount to a supplier cartel and may be a means of dealing with the suppliers' problems rather than the problems felt most urgently by the recipients.[4]

Finally, some experts take a compromise position: the arms trade is a secondary rather than a primary cause of conflict. It may exacerbate tensions in the region, spur an arms race, make war more likely, or either hamper or facilitate conflict resolution. Arms transfer controls focused on a certain region, certain weapon types, or a particular time or place are the suggested course.[5]

As with any arms transfers, it is impossible to a provide a simple or definitive assessment of Russian arms transfers to East Asia. There are many dimensions to take into account, including the security implications of Russian arms transfers for interstate relations at three levels—bilateral, regional and global—discussed in sections II–IV. Section V presents the conclusions that may be drawn from this study.

II. Bilateral relations

It is usually assumed that recipient governments are likely to be influenced by their main arms suppliers, even more so if they have only one main supplier.[6] However, empirical evidence of this effect is difficult to find—in the case of Russian arms transfers to East Asia for five main reasons. First, Russia is too weak to exert real influence on its arms recipients. While the USSR used to combine arms transfers

and its Implications for the International System (Princeton University Press: Princeton, N.J., 1987), pp. 394, 405–407.

[4] Gompert, D. and Vershbow, A., 'Introduction: controlling arms trade', eds A. H. Cahn *et al.*, *Controlling Future Arms Trade* (McGraw-Hill: New York, 1977), p. 22; and Väyrynen, R., 'Curbing international transfers of arms and military technology', *Alternatives*, vol. 4, no. 1 (1978), p. 90.

[5] Brzoska, M. and Pearson, F. S., 'Developments in the global supply of arms: opportunity and motivation', eds R. E. Harkavy and S. G. Neuman, *The Arms Trade: Problems and Prospects in the Post-Cold War World*, Special Issue of *The Annals of the American Academy of Political and Social Science*, Sep. 1994, pp. 58–72; Catrina, C., *Arms Transfers and Dependence* (Taylor & Francis: New York, 1988), pp. 124–35; Kearns, G., 'CAT and dogma: the future of multilateral arms transfer restraint', *Arms Control*, vol. 2, no. 1 (1981), pp. 18–20; and Pierre, A. J., *The Global Politics of Arms Sales* (Princeton University Press: Princeton, N.J., 1982), pp. 3–5, 14–29, 278–311.

[6] Shoemaker, C. C. and Spanier, J., *Patron–Client State Relationships: Multilateral Crises in the Nuclear Age* (Praeger: New York, 1984); and Snider, L. W., 'Arms transfers and recipient cooperation with supplier policy preferences', *International Interactions*, vol. 5, nos 2–3 (1978), pp. 241–66.

Table 7.1. Russian armed forces and equipment in the Far Eastern Strategic Theatre,[a] 1986 and 1996

	1986	1996
Ground forces		
Divisions	57	23
Motor rifle	45	12
Tank	7	3
Airborne	1	1
Artillery	4	7
Brigades	2	34
Motor rifle	–	6
Artillery	–	18
Spetsnaz[b]	–	3
ATK	–	5
Airborne	–	2
Air assault brigades	2	–
Equipment		
MBTs	14 900	10 068
Artillery	10 000	11 500
SSM	363	102
SAM[c]	1 800	750
Attack helicopters	1 000	310
Tactical aviation	1 451	525
Fighters	450	125
FGA	675	300
ECM/recce	226	100
Navy (Pacific Fleet)		
Submarines	109	43
Strategic	32	14
Tactical	77	29
Main surface combatants	82	45
Minor surface combatants	136	48
MCMV	96	47
Auxiliaries	128	203
Bombers	160	60
FGA	30	34
ASW	175	122
Early warning systems/ECM	35	8
Naval infantry, divisions	1	1

ATK = anti-tank; MBT = main battle tank; SSM = surface-to-surface missile; SAM = surface-to-air missile; MCMV = mine counter-measure vessel; FGA =

fighter, ground-attack; ASW = anti-submarine warfare; ECM = electronic counter-measures.

[a] In 1986 the Far Eastern Strategic Theatre (FEST) included the Central Asian, Siberian, Transbaikal and Far Eastern military districts, Soviet troops in Mongolia, and the Pacific Fleet. In 1995 it included the Siberian, Transbaikal and Far Eastern military districts and the Pacific Fleet.

[b] Spetsnaz is the Special Forces.

[c] In 1996 the Ural MD provided air defence for the FEST.

Sources: International Institute for Strategic Studies, *The Military Balance 1986–1987* (IISS: London, 1986), pp. 45–46; and *The Military Balance 1996/97* (Oxford University Press: Oxford, 1996), pp. 115, 118.

with other foreign policy instruments, such as economic and military power, this is virtually impossible for Russia, given its domestic situation and economic and political weakness. Second, in many cases Russian arms transfers to East Asian countries (e.g., South Korea and Malaysia and some deals with China) have been determined by economic rationales rather than strategic or political considerations: Russia simply did not set out to exert influence. Third, some recipients (e.g., China and South Korea) are candidates for regional leadership themselves and would not tolerate any Russian pressure. Fourth, even Russia's relations with countries which are less ambitious in this regard (e.g., Laos, Malaysia, Myanmar and Viet Nam) cannot be described as patron–client relationships. These countries are truly independent of Russia and could easily counterbalance any Russian influence through either bilateral channels or multilateral institutions. Finally, the East Asian countries are diversifying their sources of arms in order to avoid over-dependence on any supplier.

Russia's military–technical relations with East Asian recipients can be described as more or less equitable than those of the patron–client type. The impact of Russian arms transfers on bilateral security relations can be generally assessed in positive terms. Along with the economic benefits for Russia, military–technical cooperation has helped problem solving, stimulated mutual understanding, and contributed to overcoming cold-war stereotypes and restoring security relations with former satellite states in the region (e.g., Laos, Myanmar and Viet Nam).

In particular, Russian arms transfers have made a significant impact on Russia's relations with China and had a positive influence on the domestic politics of the two countries in four main ways.

Table 7.2. Chinese armed forces in the regions adjacent to Russia, 1986 and 1996

	1986	1996
Shenyang Military Region	28	19
Armoured	5	3
Infantry	23	15
Artillery	. .	1
Beijing Military Region	30	23
Armoured	4	3
Infantry	25	19
Artillery	. .	1
Airborne	1	–
Lanzhou Military Region	14	13
Armoured	1	1
Infantry	13	12
Total	**72**	**55**
Armoured	**10**	**7**
Infantry	**61**	**46**
Artillery	**–**	**2**
Airborne	**1**	**–**

Sources: International Institute for Strategic Studies, *The Military Balance 1986–1987* (IISS: London, 1986), p. 143; and *The Military Balance 1996/97* (Oxford University Press: Oxford, 1996), p. 180.

1. They have changed threat perceptions within the political and military élites. Today, neither Russian nor Chinese military doctrine refers to threats from the 'south' or 'north'. Russia is concerned about Islamic threats from Central Asia and the Caucasus and about NATO enlargement. Chinese fears are generated mainly by the rise of Japanese military might, tense relations with Taiwan, and territorial disputes in the South China and East China seas.[7]

2. With these changes in threat perception, the two countries have made reductions in troops and military hardware in the border areas, and the configuration of the armed forces has become more defensive. Table 7.1 illustrates the reduction in the Russian forces and equipment

[7] Segal, G., 'East Asia and the "constrainment" of China', *International Security*, spring 1996, pp. 116–32; Christensen, T. J., 'Chinese realpolitik', *Foreign Affairs*, Sep./Oct. 1996, pp. 40–48; *International Herald Tribune,* 11 Oct. 1996, p. 4; and *The Economist,* 12 Oct. 1996, pp. 69–70.

in East Asia from 1986 to 1996, and table 7.2 shows the changes in China's deployments in the regions adjacent to Russia.

3. Cooperation in such sensitive fields as arms and technology transfers, conversion, military training and research, and intelligence has helped to develop an atmosphere of trust and mutual confidence and provided an additional spur to the resolution of disputes and problems. China and Russia have nearly finalized the demarcation of their border and agreed to reduce armed forces in the border areas. Chinese and Russian border guards work together to prevent Chinese illegal migration to the Russian far eastern regions and to stop smuggling. Trans-border economic and cultural cooperation between the two countries is under way.

4. The success of Sino-Russian military cooperation has reduced the influence of nationalist groups in both countries and shifted the balance in favour of more internationalist and market-oriented forces.

III. Regional relations

The implications of Russian arms transfers at the regional level are much more complicated than those at the bilateral level. On the one hand, most of the major regional actors are tolerant of Russian arms transfers to the ASEAN member states and South Korea. The only state which has apparently expressed security concerns about Russian arms sales to South-East Asia is Thailand. On the other hand, China's military–technical cooperation with Russia makes other countries in the region uneasy. They were content with Sino-Russian détente and the removal of the danger of war between the two former communist giants, but China's neighbours view the resumption of these military ties with alarm.

There are several sources of this uneasiness. Despite US assurances, East Asian leaders fear that the US withdrawal from the region will continue. This focuses regional attention on Russian arms transfers and their role in enhancing China's power. Russia is selling arms to China at a time when China is perceived as an emerging global power. Despite China's claims that it adheres to peaceful methods of conflict resolution, it has demonstrated its inclination to use force to resolve disputes with its neighbours. Finally, there is the concern that Russian arms transfers to China and to its potential adversaries—

India, South Korea, Malaysia, the Philippines and Viet Nam—could fuel an ongoing Asian arms competition.[8]

Several aspects of the current Chinese arms acquisition programmes are contributing to this regional concern. They are proceeding in an atmosphere of uncertainty and some lack of trust, fuelled by a relative lack of transparency in the region with respect to the long-range objectives and motivations and the particular force element of these programmes. This could lead to misunderstandings and unanticipated and unfortunate reactions. The offensive character of some of the weapon systems China is acquiring is also a cause of concern. Many involve offensive strike capabilities, which are the most likely to generate counter-acquisitions.[9]

In South-East Asia there is concern that China might be able to assert supremacy over the South China Sea. In East Asia more generally there is a fear of the possibility of an arms race between China and Japan in the first decade of the next century that would inevitably embroil the rest of the region.[10]

Perhaps the most concerned country is Taiwan. After learning of Russia's decision to sell Su-27 fighter aircraft to China, Albert Lin, Taiwan's spokesman in Washington, exclaimed that 'somehow, somewhere, we have to get new aircraft'.[11] The US Administration's 1992 decision to sell 150 F-16A/B MLU (mid-life upgrade) aircraft to Taiwan was intended in part to alleviate fears in Taiwan.[12] The F-16 sale in turn strengthens China's determination to resist Western pressure on arms sales and supports the more hard-line factions set against reform and interdependence.[13] In addition, the F-16 sale—much larger than the Su-27 deal—fuelled an arms race in the region.

Officials in Taiwan believe that the resumption of Sino-Russian military cooperation could have major implications for the island. China's modern Su-27s are more than a match for Taiwan's fleet of ageing F-5E and F-104 aircraft. Some military authorities even sug-

---

[8] Menon, R., 'The strategic convergence between Russia and China', *Survival,* vol. 39, no. 2 (summer 1997), pp. 114–15.

[9] Ball, D., 'A new era in confidence building: the second-track process in the Asia–Pacific region', *Security Dialogue,* no. 2, vol. 25 (June 1994), pp. 163–64.

[10] Ball (note 9), pp. 159–60.

[11] Awanohara, S., 'Election dynamics: candidate Bush to review aircraft sale to Taiwan', *Far Eastern Economic Review,* 20 Aug. 1992, p. 20.

[12] Hickey, D., *United States–Taiwan Security Ties: From Cold War to Beyond Containment* (Praeger: New York, 1993).

[13] Segal, G., 'China: arms transfer policies and practices', *Contemporary Security Policy,* vol. 15, no. 2 (Aug. 1994), p. 168.

gest that they are superior to the F-16A/B MLU that Taiwan is buying from the United States.[14] Furthermore, the in-flight refuelling technology obtained from Russia will enable China to extend its reach to Taiwan. Hei You-long, a noted Taiwan weaponry expert, explained: 'Before Peking acquired the [in-flight refuelling] technology, only some 1000 of China's 6000 military aircraft could pose an immediate threat to Taiwan. However, with the aerial refuelling technology, which is able to increase the flight distance by five to ten times, the combat aircraft now deployed in Sichuan and Sinjiang can also pose an immediate threat to the security of Taiwan'.[15]

Finally, Taiwan has expressed concerns about the Russian defence scientists and technicians now working in China.

Japan is also concerned about China's arms purchases and has informed both Russia and the USA that it wants them to be limited.[16] Officials contend that China's acquisition of Russian arms and technology could destabilize the entire Asian region, and defence analysts warn that the strategic Sino-Russian partnership will make Russia increasingly dependent on China as a critical arms buyer. How China will behave once it acquires substantial quantities of high-quality weapons from Russia is a serious security matter. Masashi Nishihara, professor of international relations at Japan's National Defense Academy, has said that if tensions grow between the Japan–US alliance and the Sino-Russian partnership two power blocs will emerge in the region.[17]

Other Asian governments, from Singapore to Viet Nam, have expressed reservations about China's military ties with Russia. Some experts fear that increased cooperation could lead to a new strategic coalition which could threaten to isolate Japan and to neutralize US power in the region.[18] In the view of China, it has not bought more sophisticated weapons than Australia, Japan, South Korea or Taiwan

---

[14] Hickey, D. V. and Harmel, C. C., 'United States and China's military ties with the Russian republics', *Asian Affairs,* vol. 20, no. 4 (winter 1994), p. 247; and Segal, G., *The East Asian Balance after the F-16 Sale to Taiwan,* CAPS Papers no. 3 (Chinese Council of Advanced Policy Studies: Taipei, 1992), pp. 2, 8.

[15] 'Peking seen more threatening to Taiwan', Central News Agency (Taipei), 25 Aug. 1992.

[16] *Washington Times,* 19 July 1992.

[17] Richardson, M., 'A "critical moment" for security', *International Herald Tribune,* 10 June 1997, p. 7.

[18] Tow, W., 'Changing US force levels and regional security', *Contemporary Security Policy,* vol. 15, no. 2 (Aug. 1994), p. 20.

in the 1990s nor has a power vacuum been left by the USA in the region for China to fill.

The resumption of Sino-Russian military cooperation has provoked a new round of arms competition in East Asia. Whether the reaction of China's neighbours to China's arms acquisitions has been adequate is open to argument. There is a great challenge for the countries of the region and the USA to promote the responsible integration of China and Russia in the region. With a stake in the global system, the two countries would be less likely to behave in aggressive or unpredictable ways than if they feel isolated from the world community.

IV. Global relations

As with the regional actors, the reactions of the USA and some countries of the European Union to Russia's arms sales policy towards East Asia have been contradictory. Russia's penetration of South-East Asian arms markets was perceived as a challenge to the Western defence industries rather than as a serious threat to regional or global security. In response, Western arms merchants became even more assertive than before and tried to strengthen their influence in the region.

The USA and the EU countries are concerned about four major implications of Sino-Russian military cooperation: (*a*) that Russian arms transfers contribute to the growth of China's military capabilities and thus encourage its ambitions to become a dominant regional power; (*b*) that arms transfers fuel regional arms competition, which could result in an arms race; (*c*) that a Sino-Russian 'strategic partnership' could be transformed into an alliance which would challenge the existing power balance in East Asia; and (*d*) that Russian arms and technology sales may increase China's own arms export capabilities. The last point is of particular concern for the United States and other major suppliers. Many experts point out that in the 1980s and early 1990s China was the fifth largest exporter of arms in the world, supplying to many pariah states shunned by the Western world.[19] Accord-

---

[19] See, e.g., Segal (note 14), p. 157; Sismanidis, R., 'China and the post-Soviet security structure', *Asian Affairs: An American Review*, vol. 21, no. 1 (spring 1994), p. 41; Bitzinger, R., *Chinese Arms Production and Sales to the Third World* (RAND: Santa Monica, Calif., 1991); Grimmett, R. F., *Conventional Arms Transfers to the Third World, 1985–1992*, CRS Report for Congress, 19 July 1993 (Congressional Research Service, Library of Congress: Washington, DC, 1993), pp. 8–9; Kan, S., *Chinese Missile and Nuclear Proliferation: Issues*

ing to some experts, China may be acquiring Russian arms and technology for the purpose of re-engineering, manufacturing and selling weapons abroad. In 1992 the US Administration claimed that China was acquiring Russian technology mainly to develop new weapons to sell to developing countries.[20] In February 1993 CIA Director James Woolsey warned that China's acquisition of military equipment from Russia and Ukraine 'raises concern not only because the transfers improve China's military capabilities, but also because it introduces the possibility that China could, in turn, pass more advanced Russian or Ukrainian-derived technology to other states, as Beijing has done previously with its own technology'.[21]

While past Chinese arms exports may justify these concerns, some Western experts believe that the USA and the EU should not over-react for four major reasons.

1. Sino-Russian rapprochement has removed the danger of military conflict between China and Russia and the benefit to regional stability outweighs potential dangers such as the increase in Chinese military capabilities.[22]

2. Strategic convergence must not be confused with an alliance: China and Russia will not form an aggressive alliance or otherwise threaten the security of the USA and its allies and friends in the region.[23] It is more in the interests of China and Russia to maintain favourable relations with the West and with the United States in particular, because it is these relations that promise to provide the much-needed capital, advanced technology and economic partnership for economic development and growth.[24]

3. The West should avoid contributing to significant increases in Japanese, South Korean and Taiwanese military power or orchestrating an anti-Chinese coalition because this would only feed the already

for Congress, 5 May 1992 (Congressional Research Service, Library of Congress: Washington, DC, 1992); Sutter, R. G. and Kan, S., *China as a Security Concern in Asia: Perceptions, Assessment, and US Options,* CRS report for Congress, 5 Jan. 1994 (Congressional Research Service: Washington, DC, 1994), p. 5; and Gill, B., *Chinese Arms Transfers: Purposes, Patterns, and Prospects in the New World Order* (Praeger: Westport, Conn., 1992).

[20] *New York Times,* 18 Oct. 1992.

[21] Cited in Hickey and Harmel (note 14), p. 251.

[22] Menon (note 8), p. 117.

[23] Hickey and Harmel (note 14), p. 251.

[24] Ferry, W. E. and Kanet, R. E., *Russian–Chinese–US Relations and Security in the Asia–Pacific Region,* ACDIS Occasional Papers (University of Illinois: Urbana, Ill., Feb. 1997), p. 9.

substantial feeling in China that Western post-cold war strategy in the region is aimed at containing China.[25]

4. It will not be Russian arms transfers that determine whether or not China becomes a dominant regional power; rather, developments within China will be decisive.

It appears that Sino-Russian military ties and Russia's vigorous arms sales policy towards the region are a reflection of the larger issue confronting Western, and particularly US, decision makers—Russia's place in the new system of international relations in East Asia. Many Western politicians and analysts believe that the West should adjust its policy towards Russia accordingly. Some Western experts recommend that it should try to use all its diplomatic leverage to keep Russia from playing a destructive role in the region and work to restrain Russia's laissez-faire arms sales policies towards Asian states. Some moderation in Russian arms sales policy would remove a major short cut for China to acquire excessive military power.[26] Since financial considerations drive Russian arms sales policy, economic incentives should be used to curb the proliferation of destabilizing conventional arms. Using quiet diplomacy, the United States and other foreign aid donors should establish a linkage between Russia's arms and technology transfers and its access to Western aid. As Representative Howard L. Berman observed, the United States should 'pull out the stops with the Russians and Eastern Europeans and tie [its] support for their recovery to arms sales they undertake solely to generate hard currency'.[27]

It is difficult to believe that this strategy would be effective. In addition, it has become clear that Russia, both for prestige and for economic reasons, is reluctant to agree to any linkage between its arms trade policy and Western assistance programmes. In any case, it has not prevented Russia from making major arms transfers to China and other developing countries. Rather, the West should develop a general vision of Russia's role in the region.[28] As some experts recommend, Western efforts to keep a regional military balance should be supplemented by a strategy of creative engagement. China and

[25] Odgaard, L., *The Reconstruction Process of the East Asian Regional Order: The Spratly Dispute* (Aarhus University Press: Aarhus, 1997), p. 17.

[26] Tow (note 18), p. 34.

[27] Cited in Hickey and Harmel (note 14), p. 249.

[28] Harding, H., 'Asia policy to the brink', *Foreign Policy,* no. 96 (fall 1994), pp. 62, 74.

Russia, together with Japan and the two Korean states, should be drawn into a multilateral security dialogue.[29]

It appears that the Clinton Administration understands the need to adjust its policy towards China and Russia. Referring to the annual congressional debate concerning China's trading status, US Secretary of State Madeleine Albright underlined: 'Whatever the debate's outcome, China will be a rising force in Asian and world affairs. History teaches the wisdom of encouraging emerging powers to become part of international arrangements for settling disputes, facilitating shared economic growth and establishing standards of international behaviour'.[30]

At the same time, as appears from official documents, the USA continues to rely on the principles of traditional power politics and does not intend to withdraw from the region. The USA views a forward presence and the regional system of military alliances as the most reliable framework for the region's security. A 1995 Defense Department document states that bilateral treaties are more manageable than multilateral arrangements because of the diverse threat perceptions, cultures, histories, political systems and levels of development of the states in the region.[31]

However, some analysts believe that continued reliance on US security provisions forms a barrier to the development of structures indigenous to the region which could bring about a rapprochement between former adversaries, including China and Japan. Instead, there is a need for the countries of the region to promote the establishment of organizational structures which leave the discussion of urgent security matters to the regional states without the direct involvement of external powers.[32] Others regard the Asia–Europe Meeting (ASEM) process, started in Bangkok in March 1996, as a promising channel for conflict resolution in the region.[33]

Russian arms transfers have had rather contradictory implications. At the three levels of relations examined—bilateral, regional and global—only on the first was the effect clearly positive. Reaction

[29] Menon (note 8), p. 118.

[30] Albright, M. K., 'The policy is to encourage China to cooperate', *International Herald Tribune,* 11 June 1997, p. 10.

[31] US Department of Defense, Office of International Security Affairs, 'United States, security strategy for the East Asia–Pacific region', *Strategic Digest,* May 1995, p. 628.

[32] Odgaard (note 25), p. 17.

[33] Shin, D.-I. and Segal, G., 'Getting serious about Asia–Europe security cooperation', *Survival,* vol. 39, no. 1 (spring 1997), pp. 138–55.

from the actors at the other levels was predominantly negative, with the possible exception of the ASEAN countries and South Korea. A number of Russian arms transfers have had a destabilizing effect on the regional military balance and provoked arms competition. This has been the result of both regional rivalries and the lack of a sound and consistent Russian arms sale policy towards East Asia.

V. Conclusions

This study argues that Russia has vital interests in conducting an active arms transfer policy towards East Asia, primarily to support its defence industry. Russia's policy should also be seen against the background of its need to obtain hard currency to finance economic reforms (conversion among them) and ease social constraints, its attempts to develop the Russian far east, and its domestic political struggles and competition among interest groups. Important strategic and security considerations are also behind its arms sales policy. It is trying to remain an influential player in East Asia and to develop military ties with countries of the region as a strategic counterweight to a number of threats and challenges of the post-cold war era, including US hegemonism, the rise of Chinese and Japanese power, and a militant Islam.

At the initial stage, when Russia had just embarked on reforms (1992–94) and the defence industry needed immediate support, economic rationales seem to have prevailed. With time, however, Russia has managed to harness both economic and strategic incentives to conduct a more or less effective arms trade policy. Moreover, the policy has become a part of a forward-looking strategy aimed not only at the region but also at influencing the global power balance.

It would be exaggeration, however, to claim that Russia has a sound arms transfer policy, either generally or as regards East Asia. There have been some discrepancies between the ends and means as well as between the ambitions and resources. The discussion of whether arms transfers should be a major instrument of Russian policy or whether they should be subordinated to the economic and political aspects of Russia's strategy in the region is still far from concluded. Nor is it possible to make recommendations regarding how or on which principles Russia should conduct its arms export policy towards East Asian states in conflict.

The discussion on the ends and means of arms export policy is accompanied by debate on the decision-making system and the management of arms transfers. Two basic issues are central to these debates: (*a*) the extent to which the legislature and the public should control arms export policies; and (*b*) the extent to which decision-making and management mechanisms should be decentralized. In turn, these two issues reflect a more general problem confronting the Russian political system—the democratization of Russia's foreign and security policy mechanism. Whether or not Russia will be able to set up democratic principles and procedures of security policy making and establish proper institutions remains a critical question for the future of the country.

With the establishment of the independent state of the Russian Federation, efforts were made to reform arms export decision making. First, in contrast to the Soviet practices of total secrecy, some elements of glasnost have been introduced into Russian arms transfer policy. The government has released some general information on arms exports (although only on an occasional basis), and experts, journalists and the wider public have had an opportunity to discuss the issues openly. Second, a kind of parliamentary control over arms sales policy has been established. Some limited powers of oversight have been granted to a number of parliamentary committees; government agencies have begun to provide the legislature with reports on arms trade issues; and a number of investigations have been conducted by legislators. Third, the arms export control system has been decentralized to the extent that some governmental and private trading companies have been granted licences.

However, the decision-making system has proved to be ineffective for a number of reasons such as the lack of proper arms transfer legislation and effective arms export control, bureaucratic battles, inter- and intra-sectorial competition, and widespread corruption. Defence industrialists and arms trading companies have been discontent with the practices of the State Committee on Military–Technical Policy and Rosvooruzheniye. The decision-making system has been transformed so as to make it once again more centralized and less accountable to the legislature and the public. While this might make the arms export control system more effective and coordinated, some democratic principles have been abandoned in the process. The president does not want to make the parliament a full participant in the arms transfer policy-making process. Legislative checks on the executive power's policy in this field are almost completely lacking. Despite the anti-monopoly rhetoric of the government, Rosvooruzheniye retains its monopoly in the arms trade. Other trading companies have not been allowed to compete with it. Information policy has again become restrictive. These developments have been typical rather than exceptional for the Russian foreign policy mechanism. The entire process of democratic reforms, ranging from the economy to political structures, was slowed down in 1993–97.

A number of obstacles appear to impede Russia's military–technical cooperation with the countries of East Asia. They stem mainly from the economic and social instability in Russia, the lack of a proper legislative basis and management system for arms exports, and differences of opinion between Moscow and the arms recipients on the methods of payment and the financial conditions of deals. None the less, cooperation has matured. Countries have become more pragmatic and more concerned with the economic than the political or ideological aspects of defence programmes. In many instances Russia has succeeded in changing the financial conditions of arms deals in favour of hard currency payments. It is learning the market rules fast and becoming a serious rival to other arms suppliers.

The security implications of Russian arms transfers to the region are the most disputed question, in both the research literature and the political arena. This study analyses the impact of Russian arms sales on three levels of international relations—bilateral, regional and global. At the bilateral level it concludes that military–technical cooperation has affected Russia's relations with recipients in a positive way. For instance, in the case of China and Russia, along with other factors, it has encouraged the two countries to change their threat perceptions, redefine their military doctrines, initiate confidence-building processes and seek enhanced cooperation in non-military areas. Although some security concerns related to future developments are still present, Russia and China do not perceive each other as constituting an immediate threat.

The implications at the regional and global levels are contradictory. Many regional and global actors acknowledge that Sino-Russian military rapprochement has removed the danger of war between the two countries and thus contributed to the creation of a more stable security order in East Asia. On the other hand, many countries believe that

Russian arms and technology transfers may enhance China's military capabilities to an extent that makes it possible for China to become the dominant regional power.

It appears that actual deliveries of Russian military equipment to the region have been much more modest than sometimes reported. The military potential acquired by China through recent purchases is still not enough to make it a leading military power in the region. It is also obvious, however, that some Russian arms transfers to East Asia have had a destabilizing effect on the regional security debate and have been used as an excuse by countries throughout East Asia to justify their acquisition programmes. This is not surprising given the low levels of trust among the governments of the region.

Russia cannot be represented as the only or the main arms supplier involved in the region or as irresponsible. Given the shrinking domestic defence markets, other major arms producers—for example, France, Germany, Israel, Italy, the UK and the USA—have become unusually aggressive and are also responsible for the arms competition in East Asia. The major causes of conflict and tension are to be found inside the region itself.

How dangerous or constructive Russian arms sales policy will be for the region will depend on the extent to which the major regional players include Russia in the evolving regional community, thus reducing its temptation to form separate strategic coalitions and play different 'geopolitical cards'.

Appendix. Register of transfers of major conventional weapons from Russia to countries in East Asia, 1992–98

This register lists major weapons on order or under delivery or for which the licence was bought and production was under way or completed during the period 1992–98. 'Year(s) of deliveries' includes deliveries made in 1992–98 only. Sources and methods for the data collection, and the conventions, abbreviations and acronyms used, are explained in the SIPRI Yearbook as well as on the SIPRI Internet site at URL <http://www.sipri.se/projects/armstrade/atmethods.html>. Entries are alphabetical, by recipient and licenser.

Recipient (R) or licenser (L)	No. ordered	Weapon designation	Weapon description	Year of order/ licence	Year(s) of deliveries	No. delivered/ produced	Comments
R:							
Cambodia	2	Mi-17 Hip-H	Helicopter	(1995)	1996	(2)	Supplier uncertain; second-hand; for VIP transport
	2	Mi-26 Halo	Helicopter	(1996)	1996	2	Supplier uncertain; probably second-hand; bought by Cambodian civilian as gift for Air Force
China	7	Il-76M Candid-B	Transport aircraft	1992	1993	7	Barter deal worth $200 m (offsets 60%); 3 more delivered to military-owned airline
	12	Ka-27PL Helix-A	ASW helicopter	1998		. .	
	24	Su-27S Flanker-B	FGA aircraft	1991	1992	(24)	Deal worth $700 m (offsets 40%); incl 4 Su-27UB trainer version
	24	Su-27S Flanker-B	FGA aircraft	1995	1996–97	24	Deal worth $2.2 b; incl 6 Su-27UB trainer version

No.	Designation	Description			No. delivered	Comments
2	Su-27UB Flanker-C	FGA/trainer aircraft	1992	1992	2	Original order for 12 Su-27 fighter aircraft reduced to 2 Su-27UB trainer version
4	AK-130 130mm	Naval gun	1996		..	On 2 Sovremenny Class destroyers
(15)	SA-15 SAMS	AAV(M)	(1996)	1997	(15)	
(1)	36D6 Tin Shield	Surveillance radar	1992	1993	(1)	For use with SA-10c/ S-300PMU SAM systems
(1)	76N6 Clam Shell	Surveillance radar	1992	1993	(1)	For use with 4 SA-10c/ S-200PMU SAM system
4	Bass Tilt	Fire control radar	1996		..	On 2 Sovremenny Class destroyers; for use with AK-630 30mm guns
12	Front Dome	Fire control radar	1996		..	On 2 Sovremenny Class destroyers; for use with SA-N-7 ShAMs
2	Kite Screech	Fire control radar	1996		..	On 2 Sovremenny Class destroyers; for use with AK-130 130mm guns
6	Palm Fond	Surveillance radar	1996		..	On 2 Sovremenny Class destroyers
(4)	SA-10d/S-300PMU-1	SAM system	1992	1993–97	(4)	Number delivered could be 6
4	SA-N-7 ShAMS/Shtil	ShAM system	1996		..	On 2 Sovremenny Class destroyers
2	SS-N-22 ShShMS	ShShM system	1996		..	On 2 Sovremenny Class destroyers
2	Top Plate	Surveillance radar	1996		..	On 2 Sovremenny Class destroyers
(288)	AA-11 Archer/R-73	Air-to-air missile	(1991)	1992	(144)	For 24 Su-27 fighter aircraft
(48)	AA-8 Aphid/R-60	Air-to-air missile	1991	1992	(48)	For 24 Su-27 fighter aircraft
(288)	AA-11 Archer/R-73	Air-to-air missile	1995	1996	(288)	For 24 Su-27 fighter aircraft

Recipient (R) or licenser (L)	No. ordered	Weapon designation	Weapon description	Year of order/ licence	Year(s) of deliveries	No. delivered/ produced	Comments
	(144)	SA-10 Grumble/5V55R	SAM	1992	1993–97	(144)	For 4 SA-10d/S-300PMU SAM systems
	(255)	SA-15 Gauntlet/9M330	SAM	(1996)	1997	(255)	For SA-15 SAM system
	(88)	SA-N-7 Gadfly/Smerch	ShAM	1996		..	For 2 Sovremenny Class destroyers
	(30)	SS-N-22 Sunburn/P-80	ShShM	1998		..	For 2 Sovremenny Class destroyers
	2	Kilo Class/Type-636E	Submarine	1993	1997–98	2	
	2	Kilo Class/Type-877E	Submarine	1993	1995	2	Originally built for Poland and Romania but cancelled
	2	Sovremenny Class	Destroyer	1996		..	Originally ordered for Soviet/Russian Navy, but cancelled before completion; deal worth $500 m
North Korea	15	Drum Tilt	Fire control radar	(1979)	1992–94	(3)	For 15 Soju Class FAC; for use with 30mm guns
	5	Drum Tilt	Fire control radar	(1987)	1993–95	(3)	For Taechong-2 (Mayang) Class patrol craft
	(15)	SS-N-2 ShShMS	ShShM system	(1979)	1992–94	(3)	For 15 Soju Class FAC
	15	Square Tie	Surveillance radar	(1979)	1992–94	(3)	For 15 Soju Class FAC; supplier uncertain
	6	Square Tie	Surveillance radar	(1979)	1993	(1)	For 6 Sohung Class FAC; supplier uncertain
Malaysia	18	MiG-29S Fulcrum-C	FGA aircraft	1994	1995	18	Deal worth $600 m (offsets $220 m incl $150 m

	(216)	AA-11 Archer/R-73	Air-to-air missile	1994	1995	(216)	barter); incl 2 MiG-29UB trainer version; Malaysian designation MiG-29N. For 18 MiG-29SE FGA aircraft
	(96)	AA-12 Adder/R-77	Air-to-air missile	(1997)		..	For 16 MiG-29S FGA aircraft
Myanmar	5	Mi-17 Hip-H	Helicopter	1996	1997	(5)	
	7	Mi-17 Hip-H	Helicopter	1995	1995	7	
Philippines	20	Yak-18T	Light aircraft	(1993)	1994–96	(20)	
Singapore	350	SA-16 Gimlet/Igla-1	Portable SAM	1997	1998	(350)	Deal incl also 30 launchers; option on 500 more
South Korea	(33)	BMP-3	IFV	1995	1996–98	(33)	Part of payment for Russian $210 m debt to S. Korea; incl for Marines; number delivered could be up to 70
	(33)	T-80U	Main battle tank	1995	1996–97	33	Part of payment for Russian $210 m debt to S. Korea; number delivered could be 80
	(528)	AT-10 Bastion/9M117	Anti-tank missile	1995	1996–98	(528)	For BMP-3 IFVs
	(396)	AT-11 Sniper/9M119	Anti-tank missile	1995	1996–97	(396)	For 33 T-80U tanks
	(45)	AT-7 Saxhorn/9M115	Anti-tank missile	1995	1996	(45)	Part of payment for Russian $210 m debt to S. Korea; for technical evaluation
	(45)	SA-18 Grouse/Igla	Portable SAM	1995	1996	(45)	Part of payment for Russian $210 m debt to South Korea

Recipient (R) or licenser (L)	No. ordered	Weapon designation	Weapon description	Year of order/ licence	Year(s) of deliveries	No. delivered/ produced	Comments
L:							
China	(200)	Su-27SK Flanker-B	FGA aircraft	1996	1997	(21)	Incl assembly from kits; Chinese designation J-11
North Korea	(100)	SA-16 Gimlet/Igla-1	Portable SAM	(1989)	1992–96	(100)	
	(800)	SA-7 Grail/Strela-2	Portable SAM	(1985)	1992–93	(200)	

Note: In the column *Weapon designation*, the Russian weapon systems are given with both the US or NATO codenames and the Russian names to facilitate their identification, since both names are used in the literature.

Source: SIPRI arms transfers database.

Abbreviations and acronyms

AAV	Anti-aircraft vehicle
FAC	Fast attack craft
FGA	Fighter/ground attack
IFV	Infantry fighting vehicle
incl	Including/includes
(M)	Missile-armed
mm	Millimetre
SAM	Surface-to-air missile
ShAM	Ship-to-air missile
ShShM	Ship-to-ship missile
ShShMS	Ship-to-ship missile system
VIP	Very important person

Conventions

. .	Data not available or not applicable
( )	Uncertain data or SIPRI estimate
b	billion (10^9)
m	million (10^6)

Index